# MY
# HOST
# THE
# WORLD

Volume III of Persons and Places

*by* George Santayana

**M**y *Host the World* was the last thing Santayana wrote. This volume brings to its conclusion what may well be one of the great autobiographies. It concludes also the life-work, in thought and in letters, of one who was a master. Santayana has written of himself, "For my own part, I was certain that life was not worth living; for if religion was false everything was worthless; and almost everything if religion was true . . . but I was never afraid of disillusion, and I have chosen it." Throughout that disillusion-ment this has always been his greatest need. It is a book charged with the presence of a unique human being, written with characteristic humor, insight, wit, imaginative perception and beauty of phrasing, and packed with the wisdom and achieved serenity of a philosopher and poet toward the close of a long and deeply lived experience of life.

## By George Santayana

PERSONS AND PLACES: THE BACKGROUND OF MY LIFE
THE MIDDLE SPAN: VOL. II OF PERSONS AND PLACES
MY HOST THE WORLD: VOL. III OF PERSONS AND PLACES
DOMINATIONS AND POWERS: REFLECTIONS ON LIBERTY, SOCIETY
    AND GOVERNMENT
THE IDEA OF CHRIST IN THE GOSPELS, OR GOD IN MAN
REALMS OF BEING
THE REALM OF SPIRIT
THE REALM OF TRUTH
THE PHILOSOPHY OF SANTAYANA: SELECTIONS FROM THE WORKS
    OF GEORGE SANTAYANA
OBITER SCRIPTA: LECTURES, ESSAYS AND REVIEWS
THE LAST PURITAN: A MEMOIR IN THE FORM OF A NOVEL
SOME TURNS OF THOUGHT IN MODERN PHILOSOPHY
THE GENTEEL TRADITION AT BAY
THE REALM OF ESSENCE
THE REALM OF MATTER
PLATONISM AND THE SPIRITUAL LIFE
DIALOGUES IN LIMBO
POEMS
SCEPTICISM AND ANIMAL FAITH
EGOTISM IN GERMAN PHILOSOPHY
SOLILOQUIES IN ENGLAND AND LATER SOLILOQUIES
CHARACTER AND OPINION IN THE UNITED STATES
THE SENSE OF BEAUTY
INTERPRETATIONS OF POETRY AND RELIGION
THE HERMIT OF CARMEL AND OTHER POEMS
WINDS OF DOCTRINE
THE LIFE OF REASON: OR THE PHASES OF HUMAN PROGRESS

    I.  Introduction and Reason in Common Sense
   II.  Reason in Society
  III.  Reason in Religion
  IV.  Reason in Art
   V.  Reason in Science

LITTLE ESSAYS DRAWN FROM THE WORKS OF GEORGE SANTAYANA
By Logan Pearsall Smith, *with the collaboration of the author*

## *Charles Scribner's Sons*

# MY HOST THE WORLD

GEORGE SANTAYANA

As drawn from life by
Lino S. Lipinsky, in Rome, 1950.

# MY HOST THE WORLD

## GEORGE SANTAYANA

VOL. III ✻ *Persons and Places*

*NEW YORK*
CHARLES SCRIBNER'S SONS
1953

COPYRIGHT, 1953, BY
CHARLES SCRIBNER'S SONS

Printed in the United States of America

A

# CONTENTS

# MY HOST THE WORLD

# CHAPTER I

## A CHANGE OF HEART

IF a man were a wild spirit without a body or a habitat his philosophy might harmlessly change at every moment, and he might well pride himself on changing it often and radically, so as to display fertility of spirit and enjoy an inexhaustibly rich experience. Being absolutely free and unfettered by circumstances, why should he stick to any particular principles or ideas and waste his time repeating himself like an idiot or a cuckoo?

It happened in my case, however, that I reached the age of reflection in Avila, a little walled city, where old people, old churches, and barren grey moors strewn with prehistoric boulders filled my mind from the first with a sense of antiquity. Nor did reflection later, in the New World, lead me seriously to think myself, or anyone else, a disembodied spirit. On the contrary, it seemed to me evident that no discoverable mind can ever have existed except in a body; so that by the presence and action of that body it might give signs and leave memorials of its passage. Then the past might be partly recalled on occasion, not as a vain dream, but as an experience and a lesson still applicable to a moderately stable world. Moreover, this stable world might contain other living bodies, similar to one's own; and their action and gestures, by mimicry, might instantly suggest to us desires and intentions animating those creatures, and rendering them sympathetic or hostile to ourselves; and so a moral world, practical and social, would become, for our imagination, the theatre of our action, and a roughly valid representation of the forces actually playing upon us and determining the weal and woe of our lives.

On the other hand, the true romantic genius who to-day cries to the West Wind "Be thou me, impetuous one!" will cry no less

I

exultantly tomorrow to become the East Wind for a change: although in infinite vacancy it might be hard to find the difference. A truly free spirit will never repent; he cannot revert to his true self, since he has no particular self to revert to. He must simply go on, as transcendental spirit actually does, from one fresh incarnation to another, in and out forever of every living thing. He must will everything, do everything and suffer everything, but his spirit can never die: at least it can never prevent itself from being born again. It must lust forever after the Eternal Feminine, or to put it more crudely, after the female of every species.

As for me, not only my body but my rather special and difficult relations to persons and places seemed clearly imposed facts; and in that setting my personal tastes and feelings became early apparent, and caused me to feel that I lived in a kind of solitude, not transcendental and spiritual, but decidedly solitariness in a crowd and foreignness among very distinct people. My preferences were clearly marked and out of harmony with my surroundings and, as I soon felt, with my times. But conceit, or firmness of disposition, kept me from suspecting that I ought to change my allegiances, and think and feel, play and work, as did the majority. Nor did I feel any impulse to contradict them or blame them. I had nothing to complain of, but I preferred solitude.

There was therefore no occasion for me to suffer moral revolutions or undergo any radical change of heart. My interest in religion had never been agonising, only speculative and devotional. Nothing in me called for any conversion or *metanoia*. Time might transmute, without erasing, my first opinions and affections; I might wish to change my surroundings and my way of living; I never undertook to change myself. I regard my occupations and interests somewhat as an actor regards his various parts or a painter his subjects. That a man has preferences and can understand and do one thing better than another, follows from his inevitable limitations and definite gifts; but that which marks progress in his life is the purity of his art; I mean, the degree to which his art has become his life, so that the rest of his nature does not impede or corrupt his art, but only feeds it.

Now in my mental life there have been two great impediments, two congenital vices, two initial temptations; the temptation of the primitive poet to believe his fables, and the temptation of the spontaneous agent to lose himself in his world. The primitive poet falls into that first temptation inevitably; his inspiration is passive and not an art; he lends credence to his obsessions as to a higher kind of knowledge, and proclaims each new intuition to be a revelation of the truth. The Jews, says Spinoza, whenever they think something, say God told them. Prophets indeed do this explicitly and with full conviction, opposing their sudden intuitions to the current views of mankind. They are even more credulous and absorbed in life than are ordinary people, only in some extraordinary direction. Yet, unlike madmen, good prophets proclaim new ideas that the world can be led to take seriously and to weave into its conventions, at least for a time and in some sect; whence all traditional religions and moralities.

I am naturally incredulous and not a willing dupe of life in the world or in my own head; yet my imagination is not inactive. I am therefore a sort of prophet at second hand, appreciating the inspiration of others and enjoying it as my own; and for that reason the temptation to mistake it for revelation was in my case never invincible. I have said how my youthful piety was accompanied by an equal delight in geography and in architecture. I had little real contact with any of these things, but pure delight in the form and idea of them. All that I later clearly denied them was the assent due to matters of common knowledge or history: matters of fact important to get right in action, but not especially interesting to the imagination of a poet.

All her life my sister Susana was a little troubled because, as she said, she feared that I was "moving away from God." Yet at heart I was not *moving* at all. I was only *seeing* what a catastrophe the Christian *Weltanschauung* was pregnant with, if you took it for history and cosmology, and not for a symbolic myth. And this intellectual catastrophe would also involve a moral one, in that it implied the exhaustion of an inspiration, the decay of a *Kultur*. It would be comparable to the catastrophe of paganism and of the classic world, tragic but interesting. The idea of such a catastrophe caused no revolution in myself: it was more like a bereavement or a total change of surroundings. I had never *practised* my religion, or thought of it as a means of getting to heaven or avoiding hell, things that never caused me the least flutter. All that happened was that I became accustomed to a different *Weltanschauung*, to another system having the same rational function as religion: that of keeping me attentive to the lessons of life.

Each religion, by the help of more or less myth which it takes more or less seriously, proposes some method of fortifying the human soul and enabling it to make its peace with its destiny. A philosopher may perfectly well cultivate more than one *Weltanschauung*, if he has a vital philosophy of his own to qualify his adoption of each, so as to render them complementary and not contradictory. I had, and have, such a vital philosophy; and the movement of my mind among various systems of belief has tended merely to discover how far my vital philosophy could be expressed in each of them.

My variations therefore never involved rejecting any old affection, but only correcting such absoluteness or innocence as there may have been about it, and reducing it to its legitimate function. So in 1900 I published the result of the gradual transformation of my religious sentiments. Religion was poetry intervening in life. That insight had come to me twenty years before, though not expressed in those words; it had really been native to me and congenital. So when I first went to Germany and began to read Goethe, chiefly as a lesson in the language, my vital philosophy recognised itself at once in the lines:

> *Ich hab' mein Sach auf Nichts gestellt* . . .
> *Drum ist's so wohl mir in der Welt.*

This is perhaps more cavalier-like and jaunty than I was, even at that time; yet the title of this drinking-song is *Vanitas! vanitatum vanitas!* and the stanzas describe a gay fellow's discomfiture when he set his heart on money or women or foreign travel or reputation or war; so that when he repeats at the end:

> *Nun hab' ich mein Sach auf Nichts gestellt . . .*
> *Und mein gehört die ganze Welt,*

there is evidently an equivocation in his boast. The whole world belongs to me implicitly when I have given it all up, and am wedded to nothing particular in it; but for the same reason no part of it properly belongs to me as a possession, but all only in idea. Materially I might be the most insignificant of worms; spiritually I should be the spectator of all time and all existence. This implication touched the depth of my vital or congenital philosophy, and for that reason doubtless the refrain of this song became a sort of motto for me at that time. Yet more than ten years had to pass before that implication, on the emotional side, came to expression in my Platonising sonnets; while theoretically I came to clearness about it only in my old age, when I freed "essences" from the psychological net in which we catch them, and distinguished intuition from knowledge.

Clearer to me in those student days was another point. Goethe's old soldier urges us, if we want to be good fellows, to drown our disappointments in drink. But isn't drink also disappointing in the end? And if it be a solution to drink, in order to forget the vanity of life and incidentally the vanity of drinking, wouldn't it be a better and juster solution to live in general as the world lives, so as to forget the vanity of doing so? Didn't all my American friends endeavour, with a good conscience, to drown unhappiness in work? Wasn't there some intoxication also in wealth, in women, in travel, in fame, and in war? And if drink and comradeship have a good side, which makes them jolly even if vain, have not all those other vanities their good side also? To abuse them satirically, out of spite, because you had expected too much of them, would be merely childish or, if you like, romantic. It would prove you to be moody, ill-bred, and unphilosophical.

Being a philosopher, I couldn't accept a solution not based on the truth. If all is vanity—and I heartily agreed to that—the solution must be built on remembering that fact, not on forgetting it; and if drinking and comradeship have a good side—and I heartily agreed to that too—the solution must recognise the good side of drink, and also of wealth, women, travel, fame, and war. Not being an old campaigner with one leg, like Goethe's soldier, but a young man just beginning to see the sunny side of life, it was more the challenge to drink that appealed to me than the chagrin at having found that drinking didn't pay. I knew that it wouldn't pay, if you gave yourself up to it; I felt no temptation to do that; but without setting my heart on anything the point was to enjoy everything with a free mind.

This was a pretty programme, easy for a boy to draw up; and my antecedent pessimism and religiosity lent a certain reality to the pose. It lay in my nature to foresee disappointment, and never to bet on the issue of any event. Yet without experience of the world, this programmatic distrust remained itself empty and insecure. Genuine detachment presupposes attachment. What can it signify for you to say that you renounce everything, if as yet you have loved nothing? I had been childishly absorbed in religious ideas, and it was a true though bloodless sacrifice for me to wash them clean of all pretensions to historical or material truth; yet I was able to do so when quite young, readily and even gladly, because when I learned to conceive those myths as poetry, their meaning and beauty, far from being lost, seemed to me clearer and more profound than ever.

The problem was not so easily solved when it came to exorcising the world and freeing myself from all illusions about it. The world is not a myth, to be clarified by a little literary criticism. It envelops our substance with a kindred substance immensely more voluminous; it stimulates and feeds from every quarter the concupiscence of the flesh, the concupiscence of the eye, and the pride of life. What can the poor rush-light of spirit, kindled in the midst, do to clarify them? The aspiration and the desire must be accepted for the performance.

That nevertheless, as a sentiment, my eventual *metanoia* was sincere may be seen in the slow change that appeared in my way of living. Old age contributed to it; on the other hand, I had larger means and easier access to the great world, had I been in love with it. But I have ultimately become a sort of hermit, not from fear or horror of mankind, but by sheer preference for peace and obscurity. Fortune has become indifferent to me, except as fortune might allow me to despise fortune and to live simply in some beautiful place. I have cut off all artificial society, reducing it to the limits of sincere friendship or intellectual sympathy. Instead of collecting pictures and books, as I had a tendency to do in the early 1890's, I have distributed my few possessions, eschewed chattels of every kind, a fixed residence, servants, carriages, or anything that would pin me down materially or engulf me in engagements. I have indulged rather freely at certain times in good food and good drink; but I think the glamour of those pleasures was due almost entirely to conviviality, that is to say, to a momentary imitation of friendship. In themselves, when I was alone, food and drink were never important to me. I was almost happier when I could be frugal, as at my father's at Avila, in the Duval restaurants in Paris, in the teashops in London, or now, where I write these words, under the drastic restrictions of war, in the clinic of the Blue Sisters upon the Caelius. I am happy in solitude and confinement, and the furious factions into which the world is divided inspire hatred for none of them in my heart.

It should be normal, at least according to the ancients, for a philosopher to reach this moral settlement in old age; but why did the idea of it and the need of it come upon me powerfully at the age of thirty? There were various reasons. For a poet and a lover of youth the age of thirty is itself a ground for *metanoia*. Being a teacher had been forced upon me by the necessity of somehow earning my living; but being a student was my vocation, and I had been living among students, interesting myself in their sports and their pleasures, and loving their quick and unprejudiced minds. Still this second vicarious adolescence had a rift in it: my sympathy with the young and theirs with me had limits that were growing narrower and sharper. My young friends seemed to me every year younger and younger, more and more standardised and generic. They would no longer be my friends, but only boys at the school where I happened to be one of the masters. That chapter then had come to an end: yet youth, in the world and in the poet's eyes, is perpetual. The platonic transition was therefore at once spontaneous and inevitable, from the many to the one, from the existent but transitory to the ideal and eternal.

This transition may be called philosophic *metanoia*. Like the tragic catharsis, it turns disaster into a kind of rapture without those false comforts and delusions by which religious *metanoia* is often cheapened. This philosophic insight was now brought home to me by the unexpected death of Warwick Potter. Though seven years younger than I, he had been a real friend, and as I now felt, my *last* real friend. I have already mentioned that I was surprised by the effect that the news of his death had upon me. Why did it move me so much? Though he was a general favourite and a long procession of us walked behind the bier at his funeral, there was after all nothing extraordinary about him. The cause of my emotion was in myself. I was brimming over with the sense of parting, of being divided by fortune where at heart there was no division. I found myself, unwillingly and irreparably, separated from Spain, from England, from Europe, from my youth and from my religion. It was not good simple Warwick alone that inspired my verses about him. It was the thought of everything that was escaping me: the Good in all the modes of it that I might have caught a glimpse of and lost.

Another event that same year had helped to *disintoxicate* my mind: the death of my father. I had never before seen anyone die, and that in itself is an impressive and sobering experience.

We were not at best an affectionate family, and my father had not
had severe suffering to endure, yet the circumstances were deeply
pathetic. He was seventy-nine years old, deaf, half-blind, and
poor; he had desired his own death and had attempted to hasten it.
The fact that he was my father, whose character and destiny were
strikingly repeated, with variations, in my own, called up a lurid
image of what my life in the world was likely to be: solitary,
obscure, trivial, and wasted. I must not look ahead. Ahead, after
youth was gone, everything would grow sadder and sadder. I must
look within or above. I must follow the counsel that Beatrice gives
to Dante, when she sees him overcome with repentance for his
vain life in the world:

> Pon giù'l seme del piangere, ed ascolta,*

Drop (false hopes) the seed of tears, and listen. Listen to reason.
If the joys of youth and the vision of perfect love have faded from
your world, will you allow any baser thing to fetter you there?
Let your heart rather follow its true object where that object is
gone, into eternity.

A third event, the year before, had struck perhaps even deeper
into my conscience. I had seen the illusion in disillusion, the
vanity of religious substitutes for earthly happiness. In recording
"Changes in Avila" I have said something about my sister's marriage. "Marriage and death and division," said the coxcomb Swinburne, "make barren our lives." Marriage properly makes our lives
the opposite of barren; but it was not in the spontaneous ardour
of youth, with the prospect of helping to people the world, that
my sister had married: she was forty-one years old, and her husband already had six children. Nor was marriage in her case going
to separate her from anything or anybody: she had no satisfactory
friends or relations, and it was from loneliness that she was taking
refuge in the difficult position of stepmother. Nor did her marriage divide her materially from me. On the contrary, it gave me,

* Purgatorio, XXXI, 46, et seq.

just when my father's life was closing, a fresh and agreeable home in Avila, where I could make her and her new family long visits. Why then did her marriage displease and dishearten me? Because it seemed, in such unfavourable circumstances, an act of desperation on her part, a redoubled proof of her weakness. She explained it by saying that she needed affection; but a second, semi-foreign wife and stepmother would surely find more criticism than affection in her new family. It was not the sweetness of affection actually found that attached her to them, or the prospect of a peaceful home life. I couldn't help seeing that it was a craving for moral support and social backing in her religion and in her self-esteem: the backing of poor dear little old Avila! This thought distressed me. When she had entered her convent in Baltimore, little poetry or dignity as there might be there, I had admired her courage in showing what seemed such contempt of the world. The material separation between us would then have been complete, but the sense of spiritual sympathy more than outweighed it. Her leaving the convent later was no surprise; she had attempted too much and too late; but her marriage now proved more conclusively that she had no contempt of the world; that her religious enthusiasm itself had been something human and social, and that she, who had given the first impulse to my speculative life, had never had any speculative or mystical insight. She was a Sturgis; and her charm and her ascendancy over me had been founded only on her natural warmth, geniality and fun, themselves now less spontaneous and engaging than when she was younger. She still clung to the Church with an intense party spirit, which she developed also in politics; but she couldn't *live* her religion as I *lived* my philosophy. It was too unreal for her human nature.

This was a sad disillusionment for me in regard to the person to whom I was most attached; and it became also in some measure a disillusionment about Catholicism. Was Catholicism, in principle, much better than Judaism? Wasn't it still worldliness, transferred to a future world, and thereby doubly falsified? The Jews frankly cared for nothing but prosperity, and their delusion was only that they could make a short cut to prosperity by smashing the Golden Calf and being faithful to circumcision and Sabbaths, or alternately by charity towards widows and orphans. In Christianity the idea of prosperity is abandoned for that of salvation in the world to come; and incidentally there is much aspiration towards spiritual perfection and many a master of it; yet this spiritual discipline is in some sense esoteric; in spite of it the goal, as conceived by the materially pious, remains as with the Jews an impossible security amid impossible splendours. The incidental esoteric discipline, which is all that I respect in Catholicism, terminates in the same inward liberation and peace that ancient sages attained under all religions or under none. The question is whether the paraphernalia of salvation are not in all cases accidental, sometimes pleasing and poetical, sometimes dangerously superstitious; and whether they do not encumber the spirit with other-worldliness.

Here, then, were four thoughts merging their currents and carrying me irresistibly towards the same sea: youth was past, friendship had had its day, the future offered me nothing that I cared for, religion and social utopias proposed nothing that I respected. I was driven from the temporal to the eternal, not by any one crisis or conjunction of events, but by the very nature of existence, when this had been honestly faced and frankly admitted. The cry of Ecclesiastes, *Vanitas vanitatum*, could be re-echoed, and the motto from Goethe about setting my heart on nothing could be retained; but both in a new spirit. At twenty my empty spleen could make a clean sweep of the world beforehand, because nothing in it would last forever; it didn't occur to me to ask whether lasting forever would improve anything that was worthless while it lasted. But ten years later I had travelled. I had learned something of the pleasures and manners of mankind, and for myself I had made some progress in the primrose path of Epicurean wisdom. I had now forever in my fancy a lovely picture of ancient Greece and a lovely picture of modern England;

and having begun by fully admitting that all was vanity, I could not be angry with the primroses for fading or with the path for being short. I accepted them as vain but beautiful, transitory but perfect; and I was no less ready to enjoy them than to give them up. To give them up, I mean, as possessions, as enjoyments, as private hopes; I would never give them up as allegiances. Never should I esteem and love them less because they happened to pass out of my orbit.

In another field, not so strictly personal, I was compelled to accept a rather difficult renunciation. I was a teacher of philosophy in the place where philosophy was most modern, most deeply Protestant, most hopefully new!—the very things from which, in speculation, my *metanoia* turned me away. I could never be, I will not say a leader, but even a happy participator in the intellectual faith of my neighbours. Not that I had any hostility to that faith: it was as natural in its place and time as any other, and contained important elements of truth; but it could never be my faith. In the midst of the living, I could live only with the dead. It was a comfort, but a cold comfort, to say that I was living among the immortals.

Reacting now against all these closed doors, I found the moral of Goethe's drinking-song cheap and hollow. His old soldier *dishonours* his past, as if his present cynicism and rowdiness could be something better. This is only one more mood, one more incident, and a more vulgar one because there is less courage in it. There was vitality in those human adventures; there is also wit and good humour in laughing now at their seamy side; but it is dishonourable and self-contradictory to forswear your honest loves, past or present. They it is that reveal your true nature and its possible fulfilments; they are the Good, in the modes of it that you can appreciate and unfeignedly worship. There is therefore enthusiasm no less than resignation in an enlightened *metanoia*. You give up everything in the form of claims; you receive everything back in the form of a divine presence.

This final settlement of the moral problem involved no visible change in my mode of living. I went on teaching and writing, drinking and travelling and making friends; only that now, beforehand and explicitly, these occupations were marked for me with a cross: the sign on the one hand of death and on the other of consecration. Gradual and bloodless as the change was, there was a wrench in it, a passage through dark night. I had become aware that, as a spirit, I was not myself but pure spirit, to whom all selves are mere objects, and all their joys and sufferings so many animal vapours, to be endured courageously and no less courageously dismissed and wiped away. The truth of life could be seen only in the shadow of death; living and dying were simultaneous and inseparable. For, as Emerson has it,

> This losing is true dying,
> This is lordly man's down-lying,
> This his true and sure declining,
> Star by star his world resigning.

Yet this transit through darkness brought me quickly back into the light, into the pure starlight that transports without dazzling. No part of time is lost in eternity, only the haste and uncertainty of passing from one thing to another. I had not been ravaged by any hostile fate; my heart had simply uttered a warning against its own weakness. It had said to me: Cultivate imagination, love it, give it endless forms, but do not let it deceive you. Enjoy the world, travel over it, and learn its ways, but do not let it hold you. Do not suffer it to oppress you with craving or with regret for the images that you may form of it. You will do the least harm and find the greatest satisfactions if, being furnished as lightly as possible with possessions, you live freely among ideas. To possess things and persons in idea is the only pure good to be got out of them; to possess them physically or legally is a burden and a snare.

I know very well that this philosophic salvation is not such as nature or life looks for or can accept: it is only what the truth affords to the spirit. Life and nature do not ask to be saved from themselves: they ask only to run on at full tilt. It is the spirit that asks to be saved from that insane predicament. Yet spirit is an emanation of life, and it is more truly and naturally happy in the first phases of its career than in its final salvation. In the end, when it has understood and renounced everything, if you ask it whether it is happy, it can reply only as La Vallière replied to the friends who asked her if she were happy in the Carmelite convent to which she had retired: *Je ne suis pas heureuse; je suis contente*. Nature had been muted, but spirit had been freed. In that sense, and under the spell of that profound conviction, I composed the second sequence of my sonnets, using the traditional language and images of love which can render that sentiment best. They belong to a second-rate kind of poetry that in itself has no claim to attention; but here, considered as autobiography, they may be recalled. The key to the whole is given in the one line:

*A perfect love is founded on despair*

This paradox is condensed and rhetorical; to get at the truth in it we must expand it a little and ward off certain misunderstandings. It is not love simply, but only *perfect* love that includes despair. Love in itself includes hope, or at least a desire to preserve the object of it, to enshrine and defend it. And in regard to the object even perfect love retains this solicitude. It is only in regard to the lover, as a poor human being, that hope must be cut off, plucked up by the roots, if love is ever to become pure, happy, and immortal. The perfect lover must renounce pursuit and the hope of possession. His person and life must, in his own eyes, fall altogether out of the picture. Stendhal, in his book *De l'Amour* (which unlike his others pleases me very much) distinguishes four kinds of love, *l'amour physique, l'amour vanité, l'amour goût,* and *la grande passion*. The first two are obviously imperfect and impure: they include craving, jealousy, cruelty, fear, folly, and self-degradation. Yet the vital side of physical love cannot be dispensed with, since it is the root of the whole growth and most intense in the *grande passion*. In the great passion this vital impulse is often diverted from physical lust and jealousy to absolute devotion, heroism and suicide. It is therefore psychologically not only possible but normal for the passion of love to be self-forgetful, and to live on in the very act of sacrifice and personal despair. So transformed, the great passion becomes worship. And the *amour goût,* which is more playful, and turns the vital element into laughter and delight, also reaches perfection only when all thought of the self, all *amour vanité,* drops out of it, and it becomes wholly aesthetic, pure joy in beauty and charm. Combine these two elements, the tragic and the lyrical, and you have turned love into a rapture in adoration which seems to me its perfection. It presupposes the total abdication of physical, social or egotistical claims; yet these claims were instinctive in the psyche, and the spirit has either adopted them and repented, or at least felt and understood them in refusing to make them. The passion of love, sublimated, does not become bloodless, or free from bodily trepidation, as charity and philanthropy are. It is essentially the spiritual flame of a carnal fire that has turned all its fuel into light. The psyche is not thereby atrophied; on the contrary, the range of its reactions has been enlarged. It has learned to vibrate harmoniously to many things at once in a peace which is an orchestration of transcended sorrows.

# CHAPTER II

## KING'S COLLEGE, CAMBRIDGE

I FIRST went to Cambridge on a flying visit, being taken there by Russell to see his brother Bertie who, he said, was anxious to make my acquaintance. These circumstances mark, in my mind, the character of my whole connection with Cambridge, wholly different from my connection with Oxford. Bertie was then living in the new part of Trinity, small rooms in a falsely Gothic dormitory that might have been at Harvard. He was very busy; there was a knot of other friends, none of whom I remember distinctly; and I had no time to see the beauties of the place. To Oxford, on the contrary, I had gone in my first free flight, alone, and with eyes and mind open. I had at once made friends, and learned silently to thread that secluded labyrinth. Officially, I was unknown and a stray tourist; inwardly, I was perfectly at home. In Cambridge, my friends were all professional. Bertie at once became a Fellow and an intellectual leader.

Lapsley, a Harvard man of the class of 1893, later became also a Fellow of Trinity, having written a most learned work on the history of the See of Durham. He spent his life in that College, but kept up his American relations and sympathies with an admirable fidelity. To me he was most hospitable and friendly, although his intense Anglican piety acted sometimes as an ulterior barrier between us. Still, I could tell him whatever I had seen, in Spain or elsewhere, of the too human side of Catholics, and he would relish my naughtiness. Those *Romanists* were so *pagan* and their liturgy so *incorrect*! He was consumptive, and had never married. For that reason, perhaps, he was on terms of intense friendship with Mrs. Wharton and a host of other American ladies. The doctors commanded him never to skip his daily walk; and he would sometimes come to fetch me in a pouring rain which I would intrepidly face in his company, although I was not myself a slave to any regimen of exercise or of fresh air, even if heaven fall. He wondered how I could drink wine at luncheon; he drank only in the evening. But I never worked in the afternoon, I only walked or read, which I was never too boozy to do; why then not spiritualise one's mid-day food with a little liquor? It was precisely in the evening that I liked to sit alone by my fire, and perhaps concentrate my mind on something in particular.

It was in a professional capacity, as being an instructor at Harvard, that I was admitted to King's College in 1896. I was *in statu pupillari,* an advanced student, wore a Master's gown (without strings, because not a Master of Arts of that university) and dined at the high table. Never have I eaten such good food consecutively anywhere else; but it was dinner only: the rest one had in one's rooms. My rooms were first at the corner of Silver Street, and then in Free School Lane: only in the long vacation term, when Wedd lent me his rooms in Gibbs, or the Fellows' Building, did I live in the College. But what a place that was! The front or east room looked out across the Quad towards King's Parade. Over the rather bastard stone screen, you saw a picturesque row of old houses, not decrepit or intentionally picturesque: just the honestly useful, respectable work of an age of burghers. Each house was individual, but each knew and kept its place with decorum. In the middle of the Quad was a rather diminutive monument of the unhappy founder, Henry VI, adorned with two subordinate figures: Science, as the local epigram had it, turning her back to the College, and Religion, turning her back to the Chapel.

From my front windows I could see the exterior of the Chapel in violent perspective, the buttresses standing in file, like soldiers with shields, lances, and banners, or like the statue-columns of Karnak. Only a corner of the windows was visible at the top; above which the rough grey wall was crowned with lovely perforated battlements and pinnacles. Away with the pedants who say that battlements should not be perforated! Not, I grant, in a castle, although even there they may be decoratively shaped; but in a church not expected to stand a siege—the walls being all glass— why should not the traditional edging of battlements be retained for beauty's sake? And why shouldn't the compliment be paid to beauty with a frank smile, by opening lights in those mock battlements, as if they were laughing children looking through their fingers? What could be more charming and lovely than the perforated battlements and the eight pinnacles (one especially thick at the corner where the stairs wind up) of the Magdalen tower at Oxford? King's Chapel, however, has a grander air, on account of its four solid and lofty turrets. They are almost towers, yet I think more decorative than if they were towers, because more subservient and integral to the nave of the church.

And what a church! A Gothic Parthenon in dignity, a chapel only in having no aisles and only one altar; but that is the tradition proper to every temple. We can't have everything or be everything at once; the god of pantheism is a monster; and if we wish to be something perfect we must banish regret for not being anything else. Here we must banish the romantic love of unrealisable things; we mustn't ask for a forest of columns teasing us with alternative irrecoverable vistas; we must renounce a multiplicity of vaults, each higher than the other, and of galleries hanging and looking down over us, as it were, from other worlds. We must renounce the wayside shrine and the screened chapel for our tombs and our special devotions. In a word, we mustn't dream of cathedrals. This is a Gothic hall, a single chamber, and in that respect like the Pantheon, St. Sophia and the Sistine Chapel. Yet it is Gothic not only in decorative style but in structure and spirit. It is narrow, long, lofty: it draws you on, towards the goal of your pilgrimage, to the place where the altar ought to have been. It is a throne room for the Risen Christ, to be present in the Sacrament. Here concentration is perfect, the whole court drawn up in order, waiting; only the monarch is late. Meantime the arrangements continue to suggest his presence, and we may study them the more freely while we postpone our acts of homage.

In the first place, it was perhaps not altogether true that there are no side chapels. There are small chantries between the buttresses under each window, some now used as a vestry: they might have been intended to hold tombs, or even side altars. Yet these chambers are low and walled off, and may be overlooked. That which at once catches and holds the eye is the vault. It is held up, lifted up, as if it could move, like a baldachino over a procession; it is woven of intricate fan traceries, undulating slightly, without sharp arches, or heavy pendants; the fans open like palm trees from the piers, and then merge their branches in a chain of diamonds and circles down the flat central part. It is regal elegance, rather than religious mystery, that spreads this canopy over us; yet never was perspective more magnetic or vault more alive. We are in the presence of something magical, something sublime.

Nor is the Gothic charm of suggestion and interruption altogether wanting. Halfway down the nave there is a screen, with an elaborate organ above, separating us from the choir. This screen has been condemned by many critics, as interfering with the vista; but that seems to me a strange innocence. The *vista* is emphasised, almost created, by the screen: instead of one long monotonous tunnel we have a great vestibule and a great yet only partially visible sanctuary beyond. The vault is uninterrupted, the great series of windows goes round all the way, and we see the central one, with the crucifixion boldly designed, over the altar. But the altar itself, the choir stalls, and whatever else there may be in the chancel, we do not see clearly; and the aerial perspective itself is defined and the whole edifice prolonged, by the presence of that obstacle. I don't say that the organ screen in itself is suitable in style or in colour; I should have preferred a stone one with a great crucifix, as in the Cathedral at Avila; but the presence of a screen, and of a screen high, at least in the middle, is essential to the *living* beauty of the place. Pedants often hanker for a dead beauty.

The crowning glory of King's Chapel, however, is the stained glass. I believe the west window, to which one at first turns one's back, is modern, but it is not offensive: all the rest (and for once, they are complete!) belong to the period and are Flemish. Under their spell I once versified my emotion about them, and will not bore the reader by serving it up again cold. I have never studied them in detail, for their technique or the treatment of their subjects; I gazed at them only as luminous tapestry, as accompaniments and accessories: yet over their blue ground and green shadows, their heraldries, and labyrinthine figures, touched with jewel lights, my eye always travelled with pleasure. They served as a sort of opiate; yet the dreams they provoked were all of order, tenderness, grandeur, and peace.

The same qualities that appeared there in a hieratic monument, a relic of the past, appeared smiling and always young if I looked out of my windows on the other side towards the Backs. The rooms in Gibbs are the noble model humbly reproduced in Holworthy at Harvard; a large square room in front, for receiving, meeting pupils, and dining, and two narrower rooms behind, which in Wedd's apartment were one the bedroom and the other the study. This study was full of books, especially in Latin, which was Wedd's subject. But the chief attraction was the view: a vast velvet lawn, sloping gently down to the river—here more like a canal—with great avenues of trees and pretty stone bridges leading to the wooded bank and gardens on the other side. Nor was architecture absent in this prospect. To the right the lawn was bounded by the charming garden front of Clare, at once cheerful and stately, decorative and domestic. There was something, as I remember it, particularly warm and amber-like in the colour of its stone; probably the same stone that looked so granite-like in the lower parts of the Chapel, and whitened into silver towards the top. But with colour and aerial quality the English weather plays unending tricks; what you see once you may never see again, yet you may count on soon seeing something new and in some way lovely.

How was it that my heart was not anchored in King's College, where I had been lodged so grandly and so comfortably, in perfect seclusion yet with everything that I could care for within easy reach? Why have I rather clung to Oxford, where I was never an inmate? It may have been an accident. In 1897 I was not young enough to be assimilated and not old enough to count, or to become a centre for a knot of friends. I made few new acquaintances and remained generally unknown. Some of these circumstances were distinctly to my liking and others might have varied with time; yet my feeling when I was at King's was that the birds were not worthy of the cage.*

Who were the birds? The Provost—whose name I have forgotten—very civilly asked me to luncheon when I was first admitted to the College, and I never saw him afterwards. There was the antiquarian James—later, I believe Provost—from whom I might have learned many interesting things, but I never exchanged more than a few words with him. Finally, there was the notorious Oscar Browning. He openly flaunted the banners of gluttony and promiscuity, neither of them suitable for a teacher of youth; yet everybody laughed, and the authorities affected a calm indifference. He was obviously a good soul, and kind, but club-footed, fat, self-congratulatory, and licentious. His warm affections ranged from royalty to the lower decks of the Navy. He seemed to be rich; I heard that besides his Fellowship—which was permanent on the old basis—he acted as agent for wine-sellers and launched new brands of choice claret and champagne. The claret he tasted—gratis—every day at luncheon, with a mutton chop, vegetables, and a pudding. His breakfast was no less copious; and before breakfast he had bread and butter in bed with his early tea, and a special bottle of ale at 3 A.M. for which he was awakened by an alarm clock. Afternoon tea, for him, required solid accompaniments,

* The year 1896–7 seems to have been an unlucky one for finding genius at King's. Several literary lights, including Trevelyan, the poet, had just disappeared and several public celebrities, including Keynes, had not yet come up. I believe Bury, the historian, was in residence but I never came across him.

after hard daily tennis and a Turkish bath. It was he that introduced Turkish baths into Cambridge. Tea by no means took away
his appetite for dinner in hall: always a choice of thick or clear
soup, then fish, a joint, a hot sweet, a cold sweet, and a savoury,
washed down with champagne; and he with Wedd and me were
usually the only ones to have the traditional glass of port after
dinner in the combination room on ordinary days; but many others
joined us on Saturdays, when there were usually old King's men
who came up from London. With all this burden to carry, the
O.B., as he was called, seemed always in perfect health and in
jovial spirits. Was it genuine happiness, or a bold front put up to
hide a desperate misery? He was also, I should have said, an
alleged historian; but this seemed to be of no importance.

At King's I had two personal friends, Wedd and Lowes Dickinson. Wedd, who was a friend of the Russells, was my particular
mentor and guide. We sympathised in our pagan satirical view of
life. His scholarship and wit were of the Johnsonian stamp.
"There," he said once as we walked over the bridge to the Backs,
"is where the married Dons have their breeding holes." I think
he was of humble extraction, and accepted a position of Court
Fool in the learned world, with licence to say the truth in figura-
tive language. I often remembered Bangs and Barlow when I was
with Wedd: it was the same humanism without fig-leaves. Wedd's
learning was far wider and more classical, but in his person he was
less a man of the world. A little thick-set fellow with a ferreting
air, he resembled a woolly lap-dog, only black. His black hair
fell over his black eyebrows, and he seemed a picture of prehistoric man. People abroad, he would say, couldn't believe that he
was an Englishman. Once when he had mentioned his nationality
to a fellow traveller in France, the Frenchman wouldn't credit it.
Irishman, perhaps, or Welshman, but Englishman, *jamais de la
vie*. "*Mais si, Monsieur,*" Wedd protested in his perfect French,
"*Anglais piu-ah!*" I didn't say so, because Wedd mightn't have
liked it, but I think the Frenchman was virtually right. Wedd
was no Teuton, no Angle or Saxon, or Dane or Norman; he must

have been a pure descendant of the few remaining primitive Britons: a Mediterranean race! Hence our good mutual understanding.

The College was not kept open for residence throughout the long vacation; at a certain date in August I had to leave. One of the Dons very kindly gave me a list of towns with interesting churches in the Eastern Counties, beginning with Norwich and ending with Durham; a tour in that region, as yet unknown to me, would fill up my time, unless I preferred to return to Oxford where I had spent the previous summer; for paradoxically, being a member of the University of Cambridge I was not allowed to reside in Cambridge out of term, but I might reside in Oxford, term or no term. Wedd, however, had suggested that I might join him at a village near Wark-on-Tyne, by the Roman Wall, and among Roman roads, a good place for long walks; and this decided me to travel northwards, and see something of that part of England. Architecturally, the prevalence of the perpendicular was rather monotonous, even disheartening; because the Reformation seemed to have overtaken most of the Tudor churches before they had clothed their perpendicular bones with the vesture of worship, and they stand bleak and empty, like solitary dead trees. I had seen in King's Chapel the very best that the perpendicular can do, in its gorgeous intentions; it needed all the colour and all the rich accessories that the commercial wealth of the age could supply, to redeem its spiritual starkness. But at York and Durham, and especially at Lincoln, there were lovely relics of the earlier time, the castle-building age, when structure was varied, picturesque, and defiant in itself, without rejecting the splendour that heraldry and religion might introduce into it. Yet somehow the Eastern Counties, even Cambridge, have less of what I like in England, than have the South and West: they look the wrong way. They are open to the winds and to the thoughts that devastate rather than to those that fertilise and refine.

In Northumberland Wedd and I spent an austere fortnight, in a modest cottage, without baths, with food that only a good appetite could swallow, and long tramps, one day fully twenty miles, over open windswept undulating country. It is the thought of those Roman roads and fortifications, rather than the sight of them, that remains with me. The North is formless; it has spirit in it, wind, but no images that beg to be retained, sculptured, immortalised. Let the North, I say, digest its barren tempests; let it send us only its young men, the raw material of genius, for the South to instruct, to enamour, and to mature.

In sharp contrast with Wedd was my other friend at King's, Lowes Dickinson. His classicism was not of the rough, coarse, realistic Roman kind, but Greek, as attenuated and Platonised as possible, and seen through Quaker spectacles. I liked his *Greek View of Life*, but it wasn't Greek life as depicted by Aristophanes or by Plutarch; it was what a romantic Puritan of our time would wish Greek life to have been. War, lust, cruelty and confusion were washed out of it. Dickinson was super-sensitive, hardworking, unhappy, and misguided. His gift was for form; his privately printed poems seemed to me admirable; but his subjectmatter was perverse, even in those poems, and much more, I think, in his philosophy and politics. He prayed, watched, and laboured to redeem human life, and began by refusing to understand what human life is. Too weak to face the truth, he set himself a task too great for Titans: to shatter this world to bits, and put it together again on a moralistic plan. If at least that plan had been beautiful, he might have consoled himself for his practical impotence by being an avowed poet; but his plan was incoherent, negative, sentimental. It was that no one should suffer, and that all should love one another: in other words, that no one should be alive or should distinguish what he loved from what he hated.

Poor Dickinson came once or twice to America, the first time to give some Lowell Lectures in Boston. It was winter, and he suffered from the cold, as well as from the largeness and noise of the town. I remember his horror when the electric car we were in got into the subway, and the noise became deafening; also his misery when one evening we walked across the Harvard bridge, and he murmured, shivering: "I have never been so cold in my life." The cocktail, he said, was the only good thing in America. He hated the real, bumptious, cordial democracy that he found there; he would have liked a silent, Franciscan, tender democracy, poor, clean, and inspired. If he could have visited New England sixty years earlier he might have found sympathetic souls at Concord or at Brook Farm. He wouldn't have liked them, reformers don't like one another; but at least he might have imagined that the world was moving towards something better. As it was, he found that it was sliding hellwards with a whoop of triumph.

More important for me, and also in themselves, were my friends at Trinity College. Although I was a member of King's, all my work was at Trinity, under Henry Jackson as Tutor, and with Bertie Russell, G. E. Moore and MacTaggart as philosophical friends. Jackson was an influential person, he might have been Master of Trinity, the greatest position in the British university world. He was courtly, magnificent in his ample stiff silk gown, hospitable, universally informed, and learned, with the English trick of fathering some childish hobby. He maintained that Plato's logic was the same as Mill's. He was tolerant and considerate about my bad Greek, which I had confessed at the beginning; and, as I needed a translation to help me in my reading, he recommended me to get the dialogues we were to read—the *Parmenides, Philebus, Sophist,* and *Politicus*—in a cheap edition in separate little volumes with the text and a German translation on opposite pages. These little books proved invaluable. They went easily into the pocket, and I could read them anywhere during my walks, or look up again at any time a passage that had arrested my attention. He had published an analysis of the hypotheses about Being that fill the long second part of the *Parmenides.* Without attributing any historical insight to this view, I found it a useful thread through that labyrinth; and it also had an important influence on my philosophy, because it helped me to see that Being, the One, the Many, *et cetera,* were names of categories, not of existent things, so that all cosmological theories relying on dialectic (such as that of Leibnitz) were sophistical. They played with essences, and thought they were disclosing facts. Facts are all accidents. They all might have been different. They all may become different. They all may collapse altogether.

Jackson had splendid rooms in the Cloisters, afterwards occupied by Lapsley, and one day he asked me to luncheon there, to meet Lord Acton. I am not an admirer of celebrities, or curious about them. Obscure people, if they are nice, interest me much more. However, under the circumstances, it was as well for me to go. Lord Acton was a Catholic and a German; I don't know how he came to be an Englishman. He was fat, ponderous, with a full grey beard and an apostolic heaviness. His theory of history was ultra-empirical: anything might happen, and all testimony was acceptable. Miracles abounded everywhere and the testimony for prophecy, second sight, *et cetera,* was overwhelming. But even non-miraculous details seemed to fill his mind and absorb his interest. Having heard that I was at Harvard, he suddenly turned to me and asked if I knew how a certain movement had been carried out in a certain battle (which I had never heard of) during the American Civil War. The question annoyed me for various reasons. As politely as I could I said that I was born in Spain during that war, that I had heard little talk about it when I went to America, and hadn't studied the history of it. He then went on to explain the point at issue among the various witnesses, and I escaped further interrogation. The vision, I might almost say the smell, of a mind stocked like an old trunk with remnants of faded finery and knickknacks, moved me to sadness not unmixed with aversion. Daily experience, all trivial incidents floating like wreckage in a sea of ignorance, is bad enough: but think of a distinguished mind, consecrated to history, which is one of the Muses, and still remaining in that chaotic state! No wonder that Lord Acton should have felt the need of remaining a Catholic, under no matter what difficulties and sorrows! Not having found any order in the real world, he had to invoke an imaginary world where order should be morally perfect. It is a vendetta of faith against intelligence that perpetuates hostilities.

Of all my friends, of all persons belonging at all to my world,

Bertrand Russell was the most distinguished. He had birth, genius, learning, indefatigable zeal and energy, brilliant intelligence, and absolute honesty and courage. His love of justice was as keen as his sense of humor. He was at home in mathematics, in natural science, and in history. He knew well all the more important languages and was well informed about everything going on in the world of politics and literature. He ought to have been a leader, a man of universal reputation and influence. He was indeed recognised to be a distinguished man, having made his mark in mathematics and logic, and largely inspired the new philosophical sect of "logical realists." Yet on the whole, relative to his capacities, he was a failure. He petered out. He squandered his time and energy, and even his money, on unworthy objects. He left no monument—unless it be the early *Principia Mathematica* written in collaboration with Whitehead—that does justice to his powers and gives him a place in history.

In his physique he was a complete contrast to his brother, a Russell while his brother was a Stanley. Bertie was small, dark, brisk, with a lively air and a hyena laugh. According to some people he was the ugliest man they had ever seen. But I didn't find him ugly, because his mask, though grotesque, was expressive and engaging. You saw that he was a kind monster, that if he spit fire, it was a *feu-de-joie*. For so violent, so merciless a satirist, he made a charming companion. I, at least, was never afraid of him; and he was benevolence itself to the most humble and hopeless intellectual waifs. Though his laughter was savage, it was fed by the subtlest intellectual lights; that was the chief charm of his conversation, added to the sense of security that his faultless memory and universal knowledge gave in regard to any information that he might give. This information, though accurate, was necessarily partial, and brought forward in a partisan argument; he couldn't know, he refused to consider, everything; so that his judgments, nominally based on that partial information, were really inspired by passionate prejudice and were always unfair and sometimes mad. He would say, for instance, that the bishops supported the war because they had money invested in munition works; or that the United States government had called out troops, not to fight the Germans, but to support capitalism against the strikers. It was for this libel that he was sent to prison; and this wasn't the worst consequence of such rash assertions. They alienated opinion in high quarters and ruined his official career. "I would go to the stake for that," he would cry sometimes in summing up a philosophical argument. But going only to Holloway, in the first division, hadn't the posthumous value of martyrdom; and the general feeling that his judgment was unsound and his allegiance misplaced defeated all his attempts to guide public opinion.

He had been beautifully educated by private tutors at Pembroke Lodge. After the dreadful experience she had had with her elder grandson, who would throw her letters unread into the fire, Lady Russell dreaded the fatal influence of schools: Bertie at least must be preserved, pure, religious, and affectionate; he must be fitted to take his grandfather's place as Prime Minister and continue the sacred work of Reform. Bertie showed me his schoolroom at Pembroke Lodge, and his old notebooks on the various subjects that he had studied. It was perfect princely education, but a little like cultivating tropical flowers under electric light in a steaming greenhouse. The instruction was well selected, competently given, and absorbed with intense thirst; but it was too good for the outdoor climate. Moreover, there were obstacles that far from being surmounted were built upon as cornerstones of righteousness and sources of superior light. One was the hereditary liberalism and Low Church piety of the family. Another was Bertie's microscopic intensity that narrowed each of his insights, no matter how varied these insights might be, lost the substance in the visible image, the sense in the logic of the words, and made him, though he might be many-sided, a many-sided fanatic.

Bertie, Stickney and Westenholz, the three best-educated persons I have known, never went to school. Bertie, however, did go to the University, and here he made those fruitful contacts that produced his best work and opened to him an academic career. Had he been an obscure and penniless person, such a career might have fulfilled his ambition and determined his path; but for him, destined by his grandmother to be Prime Minister and by himself to be an international Messiah, academic life was but a preparation or an interlude. His vocation was to reform radically the whole intellectual and social world.

I can imagine two ways in which Bertie might have proceeded to prove how great a man it was in him to be. One would have been to carry out his grandmother's plans, get early a safe seat in the House of Commons, moderate his zeal so far as not to denounce bishops, generals, admirals or even Tory ministers, unless he had proofs of their obliquity, and generally to identify himself (as he could well do emotionally) with the official interests of his country. He would not at once or always have been in office. These intervals of leisure would have sufficed for the intensive study and the literary work that were appropriate to a leader of reform; and when his party won an election, he would have been able to exert the power of government for the heroic purpose of diminishing that power. He might have prevented the collapse of the Liberal party, by transforming it into a labour party true to democratic, anti-military, anti-imperialistic, anti-clerical principles. He might have shown the world whether at least in England it were not possible for a modern civilisation to exist with a maximum of liberty and a minimum of government.

The other way in which Bertie might conceivably have become a great man would have been by emulating people like Bacon, Hobbes, Spinoza or Auguste Comte. I don't mean in their doctrines but in their ambition. He might have undertaken an *instauratio magna* of scientific philosophy. He could have done it better than Bacon, inasmuch as the science at his command was so much more advanced; and the *Principia Mathematica*, a title challenging comparison with Newton, seemed to foreshadow such a possibility. Why, then, didn't Bertie proceed in this course? Or why didn't he choose the other, the political path?

I can judge only superficially, and from a distance. I didn't know him as I knew his brother. But judging by the work that he has actually accomplished, I think that, penetrating as his analysis might be in particular cases, in fundamentals he could never shake himself free from his environment and from the miscellaneous currents of opinion in his day. Except in mathematics, he seemed to practise criticism only sporadically, caught and irresistibly excited by current discussions. His radical solutions were rendered vain by the conventionality of his problems. His outlook was universal, but his presuppositions were insular. In philosophy he couldn't entertain the hypothesis that Berkeley, Hume, and Mill might have been fundamentally wrong. He seemed one day astonished and horrified when I said that the image of the sun as a luminous disc, sometimes (if you squint) with rays round it, was as fictitious and imaginary as the idea of Phoebus Apollo with his golden hair and his arrows. The senses are poets; and a strange allegiance to these imaginary figments kept Bertie's philosophy always inconclusive and unstable. Autobiographically, aesthetically, logically they are ultimates: they are what you confront absolutely when you concentrate and purify your attention; and in a critical analysis of experience Bertie was quite right in distinguishing them and in sticking to them. But they are the fireworks of animal sensation, not the stars of heaven. To turn them into elements in a cosmology, or into a system of ethics and politics, seems a blunder of the first magnitude. Animal sensation is sheer dream; only animal faith can lead us to reality. You can't build science out of literature; and the English and Germans, who in their positive science serve material interests and show plenty of hard sense, when they come to interpret science philosophically are crossed by the Protestant and romantic tradition of subjectivism, and end with devout feeling, translating everything into sentimental literature. Bertie at least escaped the fabulous sort of idealism. He almost emerged from psychological physics by composing physics out of logical elements. This was the "logical realism" which he took a leading part in suggesting. But he couldn't carry his suggestion out, because it dies in solipsism of the passing datum; or if you inconsistently grant many data, it dissolves into a multitude of sparks with only logical relations to one another. The universe has become a dictionary of the terms in which we apprehend it.

Less absorbing at the time, but ultimately perhaps more satisfactory, was my philosophical contact with MacTaggart. He was then a very odd person, who sidled along the street sticking close to the wall and half looking sheepishly down; and his absolute Hegelian idealism at that time prejudiced me against him. He had had, I understood, a fantastic tender passion that made him embrace some foolish illusions. But he must have seen enough in me to wish to save my soul, for he unexpectedly proposed to read Hegel with me, he an adept and I an ill-disposed outsider. It was a great favour to me; and we had a few sittings in the long vacation. We read aloud and discussed the beginning of the minor Logic, in the *Encyclopaedie der Wissenschaften*. I was then refractory to the transcendental point of view, and would continually transfer the matter in hand to the naturalistic plane, which MacTaggart, with some contempt, called *psychological*. Nothing seemed to come of our effort, and we soon gave the thing up. He retained, however, a friendly attitude towards me (as Moore did not); and during my last visit to Cambridge, in 1923, he came one evening to sit next to me at dinner in hall, and I soon found, when we began to talk about philosophy, that he had discovered that, apart from technicalities, I could be as transcendental as he. Only for me transcendentalism was a deliberate pose, a way of speaking, expressing a subjective perspective; whereas for him it revealed the metaphysical structure of all reality. He pinned his faith and hope of salvation on what I played with as an optical illusion, rendered harmless by being understood. Why didn't this mockery in me disgust and offend him? I think he was almost content with my doctrines of essence and of truth: indeed, he ought to have been more than content, because I granted much more than he asked for, at least in the case of truth. That evening he quoted me a line from one of my sonnets:

*Truth is a dream unless my dream is true*

and said that this was philosophical poetry at its best. The compliment was excessive and most unexpected; but now, on rereading that effusion of my remote adolescence, I can see that probably I then looked to the truth for the sort of *justification of faith* which MacTaggart demanded from the truth now. My imagination had framed a highly poetic, humanistic, supernaturalistic picture of the universe. I felt that it was a fiction; but I said impulsively: "If that fiction isn't the truth revealed, truth can never be revealed to the human heart." Truth was therefore—not really a dream in itself, since no mind was ever to see it—but something which it was a vain dream to look for, or to think we possessed in our philosophy.

This is what I suspect I felt at the age of twenty: but if so, MacTaggart read into my sonnet something that had never been in my mind—a perfectly legitimate use to make of words that set one thinking. For his own sentiment was different. He was an absolute idealist and could admit truth only as an attribute of opinions, more or less true as they grew more voluminous and consistent. Every philosopher thus had the fountain of truth within himself, and his system would become absolutely true if he could only make it all-comprehensive and perfectly coherent. Learned egotism could not have a more congenial prospect: but in MacTaggart I think there was also another motive force, distinctly not egotistical. Every opinion, in positing a truth to be attained, would remain essentially nothing but a dream, yet each would move truthward if it reappeared enveloped in another dream more coherent and comprehensive than itself. German philosophy is contemptuous of realistic faith in regard to perception or dogma, and of naturalism in morals; but nature takes its ironical revenge, and idealists are often most innocently realistic about society, and domestic, not to say animal, in sentiment. This definition of truth as harmony in dreams is a metaphysical echo of human craving for sympathy and democratic comfort in agreeing with the majority. We go right enough, darling, if we go wrong together!

# CHAPTER III

## *TRAVELS*

ALL my life I have dreamt of travels, possible and impossible; travels in space and travels in time, travels into other bodies and into alien minds. Not having been suffered by fate to be more than an occasional tripper and tourist, I have taken my revenge in what might be called travels of the intellect, by admitting the opposite of all facts and of all beliefs to be equally possible and no more arbitrary. These travels of the intellect helped me in boyhood to overcome the hatred that I then felt for my times and my surroundings; and later they have helped me to overcome the rash impulse to claim an absolute rightness for the things I might have preferred. Ideals are relative to the will. A little change in me would have banished that hatred and reversed that preference. My intellectual travels therefore reconciled me in the end, at least in theory, to the home facts. I could forgive the world everything except the ignorance and arrogance of thinking its condition alone possible or alone right.

In spite of my longing for unexampled things, I have always been a realist about the facts and suspicious of all desiderata and utopias. Your sanguine man who sets forth enthusiastically for El Dorado nurses a secret passion for the happy home. For that reason he is restless in his accidental lodgings and risks everything in the hope of discovering other lodgings where he would enjoy forever an unclouded happiness. The born traveller, on the contrary, is not pining for a better cage. If ever he got to heaven, on the next day he would discover its boundaries, and on the third day he would make a little raid beyond them. Imagination is potentially infinite. Though actually we are limited to the types of experience for which we possess organs, those organs are some-what plastic. Opportunity will change their scope and even their centre. The free spirit in us knows that whatsoever may be offered to it is but a reversible accident, and though we are compelled to be absorbed ignominiously in such accidents, yet the interesting side of those accidents for the intellect is only their character and their reversibility. The precision and variety of alien things fasci-nate the traveller. He is aware that however much he may have seen, more and greater things remain to be explored, at least ideally; and he need never cease travelling, if he has a critical mind.

How, being lazy and hating excitements and risks, could I de-velop this passion for travel? One incentive was aesthetic. I loved picture-books, costumes, theatres, architectural vistas, dialectical perspectives. The harmonies into which accidents could fall were picturesque; they were also ridiculous, and a sense for the ludi-crous, a love of laughter, was native to me. A kindred but less innocent motive was satirical. It was not only I, in my silliness, that was laughing at the world: it was the gods that were laugh-ing at it. Its own substance mocked the forms that it took. Not only were events and conventions mere episodes in an endless flux, but they were mechanically produced by forces irrelevant to our dramatic poses and pert egoisms: they were like patterns seen in a kaleidoscope—a toy of which I was fond. There was a sort of satirical magic in their existence, and the childish impulse was strong in me to turn the crank and see what would come next. A third motive might be found in the antecedents of my family. My father and mother had lived in exotic places. I gathered in child-hood that travel was normal and enlightening: it taught us the variety of tastes and standards in the world. My parents were nevertheless most dogmatic in their views and precise in their habits; they rejected almost everything; but this was perhaps the effect of their ill-luck. To me the existence of the things they condemned, such as religion, monarchy, luxury and fashion, was not at all disquieting. On the contrary those fancy things were fascinating, and a great relief to hear about, in contrast to the dullness of home life. I was glad to allow others to keep their ideals of any sort, provided I was allowed to keep mine. At any rate in a world where the exotic so abounded, to ignore it would be ignominious intellectually and practically dangerous; because unless you understand and respect things foreign, you will never perceive the special character of things at home or of your own mind. You will make ridiculous claims and assumptions, and you will continually run up against stone walls. *Travel,* therefore, I said to myself, *travel* at least in thought, or else you are likely to live and die an ass.

So much for the enlightening uses of travel; yet in the philosophic traveller something else is presupposed, without which he would lapse into a frivolous sightseer and his mind into an album of snapshots and clippings. Ghastly are those autobiographies that contain nothing but old jokes and old anecdotes. Before he sets out, the traveller must possess fixed interests and faculties, to be served by travel. If he drifted aimlessly from country to country he would not *travel* but only wander, ramble or tramp. The traveller must be somebody and come from somewhere, so that his definite character and moral traditions may supply an organ and a point of comparison for his observations. He must not go nosing about like a pedlar for profit or like an emigrant for a vacant lot. Everywhere he should show the discretion and maintain the dignity of a guest. Everywhere he should remain a stranger no matter how benevolent, and a critic no matter how appreciative. Were he a mere sensorium, without his own purposes, moral categories and points of reference, he might as well have left those variegated natives to lead their lives undisturbed and unvisited. They would have gone on the more comfortably without him, and he the more inexpensively without them, at home. The traveller should be an artist recomposing what he sees; then he can carry away the picture and add it to a transmissible fund of wisdom, not as further miscellaneous experience but as a corrected view of the truth.

Perhaps if in youth I had been able to satisfy my desire to travel, the lack of a fixed background, material and moral, might have reduced me to a vain wanderer. Circumstances prevented. I was tethered, even when I began to cross and recross the Atlantic, to Avila and to Boston, and allowed only an occasional halt between. My real nucleus was this combination, not easily unified. By the time I was free, I was no longer young. The Mohammedan countries, India and China, no longer tempted me. If materially I was less attached than ever to any particular spot, morally my native sphere had become definite. I was a child of Christendom: my heritage was that of Greece, of Rome ancient and modern, and of the literature and philosophy of Europe. Christian history and art contained all my spiritual traditions, my intellectual and moral language. There would have been no danger, however far afield I had travelled, of losing my moorings; and foreign things had no meaning for me except as they offered interesting analogies or contrasts for deepening my sense of my ancestral world.

This fidelity of mine to my origins showed itself indirectly even before I was able to choose my way. When in 1887 I went to Gibraltar by sea from Malaga, and saw Mount Atlas, it was the idea rather than the image that arrested me, glorious as this image was; and when I returned there in 1891, this time from America, and crossed to Tangiers with some steamer acquaintances, this first glimpse of something beyond Christendom chilled rather than excited my desire for exploration. This is the more remarkable in that one of those acquaintances was the painter John Sargent. He was then at work preparing his decorations for the Boston Public Library, and intent on finding figures and especially costumes suitable for his Hebrew Prophets; and in Spain he wished to re-examine the dressed wooden images of the Mater Dolorosa, in view of a Madonna that he meant to introduce into his design for the other end of the same hall. His appreciation of these so Spanish images appealed to me. Without being a pre-Raphaelite, he had altogether outgrown Protestant shyness in religious art, and felt the deep passion in it. Neverthless, we saw nothing in Tangiers that was more than curious: like the customs officers, three venerable old men sitting cross-legged on a raised bench, like a counter, who, having been bribed by my friends' courier, grandly motioned for our valises to pass unexamined. We saw some Jewish houses, not being admitted into the Moslem ones; and while Sargent and the others bargained for all sorts of treasures, I bought a pink-and-gold cloak, that for years afterwards decorated my wall, and that Sargent said was Venetian stuff woven with half moons expressly for the Oriental market. Two other pictures only remained in my memory of sights in Tangiers, which was then in all its primitive squalour: the market place with men, asses, sheep, and camels all lying together on the bare earth, amid puddles and rubbish; and on a slight eminence not far off, a story-teller reciting, like Homer, his military legends (so I was informed) with great calmness and long pauses, to an audience of a few scattered individuals, no less calm and otiose than himself. Yes, here was the antique background to our civilisation, important to remember; but I was sure that if we reverted to it, even as mere students and historians, it would seem tedious, filthy and trivial. In any case, I would let others inquire, and trust to their reports. Therefore, when two years later, I was again at Gibraltar, I let my American fellow travellers go to Tangiers alone, and spent a meditative day or two seeing what was to be seen from the Rock.

It was only after ten more years of routine, filled with occupations that leave no memories, that I found myself with two clear summers and one winter before me, for my first real travels. I might have gone to India, China, and Japan, had I been younger and in the mood of the Arabian Nights; but I was middle-aged and in the mood of Gibbon; *The Life of Reason* was then in the press. What a pity that I couldn't have rested and travelled before writing that book! It would have been richer in substance and purer in form. At least, I could rest now, and hope that the impurities would evaporate from my mind in the fresh air and light of history. My journey would be only over beaten paths, leisurely, comfortable, solitary, towards the fountains of my own past. I would visit, as far as practicable, the scenes where that past took shape and see *in situ* the ruins that remain of it. Perhaps this might help me to distinguish the part of my heritage that is hopelessly dead from the part that still has the seeds of the future in it. European life surely has a hereditary skeleton, an indisputable structure, that must be reproduced, of course with variations, so long as moral continuity and progress remain possible in our world.

The first scene in this drama should properly be Egypt; and from there tradition would bifurcate, one stream running to Palestine and Western Asia, the source of our religion, and another stream running to Greece, the source of our art, literature, politics, and philosophy. But the exigencies of travel and of the seasons didn't allow me to take things in strictly historical order. Tourists were not conveyed to Egypt before mid-winter, and there were side-shows, derivative episodes nearer home, that might be taken by the way. From Paris, where I had finished and sent off my last batch of manuscript, I went straight to Naples. It was September, still summer, but not unpleasant for a lazy man; and in an upper room at Bertolini's, with a wide view, I spent a few weeks of pleasant repose. I saw what was then visible of Pompeii; nothing of Herculaneum except at the Museum; and only the very surface of life in the town. But the atmosphere was already more balmy, more unconstrained, more animal, than in the north: I had moved several degrees towards the equator of the moral sphere. And not merely by way of relaxation; for I went to Paestum, and there saw Doric temples for the first time, symbols of severity, simplicity, harmony, and strength. There was the pure vein to be traced in the quartz of Roman accumulations and grossness; and I followed that vein back to Sicily.

Doric purity is not a thing to be expected again in history, at least not yet. It indicates a people that knows its small place in the universe and yet asserts its dignity. In early Christian art there may be simplicity and *naïveté*, but never self-knowledge. The aspiration in it is childlike. For anything like Doric fortitude

in the West we must look to the castles, not to the churches;
and the castles are Christian only by association. Here then was
an ultimate point of reference, a principle of manly purity, to
mark one extreme in the moral scale of all human arts, and to
give me the points of the compass in my travels. And by a curious
chance, during this same excursion to Paestum, I came upon the
opposite extreme of the moral scale also, in a form that I have
never forgotten. The reader may think it trivial, but I assure him
that to me it has the most serious, the most horrible significance.

At Paestum there was only the railway station and no hotel,
but travellers might spend the night comfortably at La Cava, not
far away. I had done so and in the morning was waiting at the
station for the train to Naples. The only other persons on the
platform were a short fat middle-aged man and a little girl, evidently his daughter. In the stillness of the country air I could
hear their conversation. The child was asking questions about the
railway buildings, the rails, and the switches. "Where does that
other line go?" she asked as if the matter interested her greatly.
"Oh, you can see," the father replied, slightly bored. "It runs into
that warehouse." "It doesn't go beyond?" "No. It stops there."
"And where does this line go?" "To Naples." "And does it end
there?" "No, it never ends. It goes on forever." "*Non finisce
mai?*" the girl repeated in a changed voice. "*Allora Iddio l'ha
fatto?*" "No," said her father dryly, "God didn't make it. It was
made by the hands of man. *Le braccia dell'uomo l'hanno fatto.*"
And he puffed his cigar with a defiant resentful self-satisfaction
as if he were addressing a meeting of conspirators.

I could understand the irritation of this vulgarian, disturbed
in his secret thoughts by so many childish questions. He was
some small official or tradesman of the Left, probably a Free
Mason, and proud to utter the great truth that man had made the
railway. God might have made the stars and the deserts and all
other useless things, but everything good and progressive was the
work of man. And it had been mere impatience that led him to
say that the Naples line never ended. Of course it couldn't run

on forever in a straight line. The child must have known that
the earth is round, and that the continents are surrounded by
water. The railways must stop at the sea, or come round in a
circle. But the poor little girl's imagination had been excited and
deranged by religious fables. When would such follies die out?

Commonplaces that had been dinned all my life into my ears:
yet somehow this little scene shocked me. I saw the claw of
Satan strike that child's soul and try to kill the idea of God in it.
Why should I mind that? Was the idea of God alive at all in me?
No: if you mean the traditional idea. But that was a symbol,
vague, variable, mythical, anthropomorphic; the symbol for an
overwhelming reality, a symbol that named and unified in human
speech the incalculable powers on which our destiny depends. To
observe, record, and measure the method by which these powers
operate is not to banish the idea of God; it is what the Hebrews
called meditating on his ways. The modern hatred of religion is
not, like that of the Greek philosophers, a hatred of poetry, for
which they wished to substitute cosmology, mathematics, or dialectic, still maintaining the reverence of man for what is super-
human. The modern hatred of religion is hatred of the truth,
hatred of all sublimity, hatred of the laughter of the gods. It is
puerile human vanity trying to justify itself by a lie. Here, then,
most opportunely at the railway station returning from Paestum,
where I had been admiring the courage and the dignity with
which the Dorians recognised their place in nature, and filled it
to perfection, I found the brutal expression of the opposite mood,
the mood of impatience, conceit, low-minded ambition, mechanical inflation, and the worship of material comforts.

In saying this I don't forget that all phases of life are equally
natural and spontaneous, and that some animals are furiously
busy while others are calm and brave. Each has its troubles and
dangers and each sometimes has its rewards. But I was setting out
on my travels with a moral personal interest, not with a scientific
one. I wished to clarify and intensify my sense of the humanly
beautiful. I wished to measure the distance and the steps between

rational life, lived in view of the truth, and blind miscellaneous living. The world has always been filled with the latter; but in classical antiquity collectively, and in modern times individually, there has been an aspiration to look before you live; and this aspiration has left traces of its passage in monuments and maxims that it is my particular desire to understand. These are the maxims and monuments of human wisdom. I had already studied the maxims; now I wished to have a glimpse of the monuments, and a hint of the conditions that had made them possible. On, then, to Sicily.

It was not yet the season for tourists and at Taormina, my first halt, I found no vehicle at the station, and when at last I got a lift in a local cart, with some difficulty I reached my hotel, where nobody was expected, and I was served with a part of my host's supper. Although the weather was good, somehow the place seemed desolate, and it was impossible to fall into the mood of luxurious enjoyment appropriate to the scene. Like Capri, where I have never been tempted to stay, Taormina seems rather a refuge for moral invalids, favourable for a long convalescence or for a slow death. I went on to Palermo. Very like a Spanish provincial city, no doubt with its special charm when you acquired a domicile and corresponding habits: but for me it proved merely the starting point for two excursions: one to Cefalù, for the sea and sunlight and the picturesque, the other to Monreale, for the Byzantine architecture and mosaics. I am no connoisseur or even amateur of the special luxurious arts, carpets, tapestry, carvings, mosaics, iron or silver work. I like it all, as I like stained glass, as an enrichment, as an element in the beauty of something greater; and such things seem to me to require the life to which they belonged, if they are not to seem mere relics, old finery looking a little childish as well as shabby in its neglected gorgeousness. Moreover, for me on this journey, the Byzantine should come at the end, in Santa Sophia.

I felt more joyful and breathed more freely, when I passed to the southern coast, and saw something Greek. Agrigentum, in its desolation, left much to the imagination, but stirred it deeply. Not so much the ruins as the magnificent site, as if all the seven hills of Rome had been linked together in a chain, doubled in height, and been made to overhang the forum and the lower town in a broad curve. That vast acropolis must have been a sublime thing. Outwards, on the convex side, it is a sheer precipice; inwards its horns descend to the plain and make it accessible. One of these horns is occupied by what remains of the town. I climbed to the top, partly by steps. There was a little square, with a café, but no vestiges of the temples that must have stood there: for a reward I saw some large white goats, apparently clean as lambs, browsing among the steep lanes or perched upon the stone enclosures that bordered them. These ancient fortresses, in the days of peace, must have been very domestic and country-like in the simplicity and monotony of their ways. Dull, except for the recurring festivals and the frequent wars, yet well fitted, in both aspects, to fix the character of tragedy and comedy, as the Greeks fixed it, limited, monotonous, liturgical, but intensely felt, profoundly human, wonderfully central and final.

Agrigentum was a colony, suddenly rich, like an American mushroom city, short-lived and ruined even more suddenly than it had grown up; but for its day it was enormous, and it gave birth to a great poet-philosopher, the literary model of Lucretius, and a grander personage, with his tragic end soon enveloped in legend. Both Lucretius and Empedocles are said to have killed themselves, or voluntarily become gods: in any case they saw the world as the gods would: that is to say, as we all should, if we could surmount our accidental humanity and let the pure spirit in us speak through our mouths. I wonder if a mushroom civilisation, by its very thinness and sudden brilliancy, like fire in straw, may not be easier for the spirit to profit by and to transcend than a more deeply rooted tradition.

My last halt in Sicily was at Syracuse, where I chanced upon a pleasant small hotel, with views towards the sea, and at once established a routine for the day, which I might have kept up

indefinitely. It was already possible for me to lead my chosen life
anywhere, provided the material conditions were favourable and
unobtrusive. I could have stayed on at Syracuse all winter. I think
it was there that I read and despatched the first proofs of *The
Life of Reason*. My daily walk usually took me to the ruins of the
Greek theatre, past what must have been the agora of the upper
town in antiquity, where the principal temple remains turned into
the cathedral. This transformation excited my architectural fancy.
To turn a Greek temple into a Christian church all you need to do
is to wall up the peristyle, leaving a window in the upper part of
each space between the columns, and then pierce arches in the
side walls of the cella. Your interior then occupies the whole or
nearly the whole of the temple platform; place an altar where the
statue of the god had stood, and you have a complete church: even
a great church, if you are prudent enough to retain a narthex
before the inner door, and an ambulatory behind the altar. This
was not done as I could wish at Syracuse; but the great columns
were not walled up so as to be wholly concealed, and the line of
the pediment remained visible, if not uninterrupted. The transformation had not been the work of one artist, but of many
bishops; yet it allows enough to subsist of the ancient temple to
make evident the continuity of worship and the identity of civic
function in this edifice for three thousand years.

What surprised me at Syracuse was the slight elevation above
the sea of Ortygia, the old castle occupied by the modern town.
I had imagined a much loftier citadel, a great marine acropolis;
but the defences must have been mainly artificial. There must
have been sea walls as at Tyre round most of the peninsula and
great towers and gates upon the isthmus. But to-day in walking
out towards the theatre or towards the northern quarters where
Epipolae extended, you hardly felt any change in height or de-
fensibility. Perhaps my expectations had been raised by the
grandeur of the acropolis at Agrigentum; I had to revise my ideal
of Syracuse, and remember that the site of Ortygia was chosen,
like that of Tyre or of Venice, for being surrounded by water,

not for being unscalable from the land: and I began a sonnet that never went beyond the first two lines, which contained all that I had to utter about these places:

> Renowned Ortygia, castle of the sea,
> And Agrigentum, castle of the air.

After this spell of solitude among ruins I returned to take ship at Naples and found myself in the social bosom of dear old Boston. Mrs. Beal, my friend's mother, was on board with a companion, and it was arranged that I should join the party. I was glad to do so. Mrs. Beal had always been friendly and confidential. I could stand for a while to her *in loco filii*; she, with her courier and maid and companion, would tell me all the facts about everything, and yet leave me free enough to observe them for myself.

We saw, during a calm voyage, the mountains of Crete, the birthplace of Zeus. Afterwards in Athens, I heard Evans, the archaeologist, talk at table about his discoveries there. Tempting from a distance, to explore those mountains and to study those ruins; yet though I felt the attraction strongly, I nursed no illusions about it and suffered only a theoretical pang at having to renounce it all. In reality, it would have been a terrible bore and far beyond my physical endurance and agility. Yet to read about prehistoric Crete excites me always, no matter how imaginative or untrustworthy the author may be. Spengler may dream what he chooses about unknown civilisations, and Racine may render mythology credible and courtly, like the myths in the tapestries of modern palaces. I like to ponder on the wonders of Crete. It was there that Plato, in the Laws, thought of founding his ideal city. In such sea-girt mountains I like to imagine it, and I repeat as an incantation, the words of Phèdre to the son of Theseus:

> Pourquoi, trop jeune encor, ne pûtes-vous alors
> Entrer dans le vaisseau qui le mit sur nos bords?
> Par vous aurait péri le monstre de la Crète
> Malgré tous les détours de sa vaste retraite.

But the monster, though he transforms his monstrosity, is perennial; and it is the pure hero, who might have extinguished monstrosity, who dies young, entangled in the monstrous luxuriance of nature, that pays no heed to perfection.

The insults with which time pursues its noblest creations appeared at once in the harbour of Port Said. I knew I was in Egypt, yet I saw nothing but huge iron freight steamers, higher than the shore, and the bustle and sordid confusion of a landing stage and a railway station. However, we were not booked to stay there, and soon found ourselves in a quiet hotel in Cairo. No distinction, no dominant character in that city; a mixture of incongruities. Only one impression, as usual architectural, remains of that week in what was and is a great focus of Mohammedan life: the one or two great mosques that we visited. It was a surprise to me, thinking of Cordova, to see them so high, so majestic. The memory of Babylon and Assyria, or the shadow of the ancient temples in Egypt itself, must have led the Moslem builders to enlarge their scale, and to be imposing; whereas the note I expected in a Mohammedan place of worship was rather that it should be secluded, exquisite and devotional. However, my acquaintance with the religious sentiment of Islam was very slight, and I procured a French translation of the Koran to read during our trip up and down the Nile.

The flat-bottomed river steamer in which I was to live for a month was comfortable, and the food satisfactory. My cabin was at the end of one of the verandahs, so that I could sit by my open door, which was also the window, and watch the river and the banks undisturbed. I made all the excursions as prescribed except one. We were to stop three nights at Luxor. On the first day I went with the rest to view the ruins at Karnak: but on the next day, when the party was conducted to the Tombs of the Kings— a particularly long donkey-ride with a picnic at the ruins—I seceded. The attraction at the Tombs of the Kings was then merely pictorial: the architecture was not important, while at Karnak I had seen one of the wonders of the world, and I wished to go again, alone and on foot, to see it at leisure. This was my

best day in Egypt. I climbed the great pylon; I wandered among
the ruins; I lingered in the great hall, trying to evoke an image
of what it must have been in its glory; I admired the minor temple
with its forecourt of colossal statues serving as columns; but most
of all I felt the spell of the inner sanctuary, approached by a sort
of labyrinth of passages interlocked, and lighted only by cracks left
purposely here and there between the immense blocks of stone
that formed the walls and the ceiling. In the inmost chamber there
was now nothing: but I could imagine the glittering antique
image that must have stood there (like the Virgin of the Pillar
at Saragossa, only colossal) which the High Priest, barefoot and
duly vested, may have approached with great ceremony perhaps
once a year. From all other eyes this inner splendour would have
been forever concealed. How profoundly appropriate, for all its
grotesque animal worship and solar myths, this ancient worship
was to the real status of man! How childish our metaphysical
moralisms and psychologisms seem in comparison!

For beauty, apart from grandeur and significance, only two or
three heads and the temple at Denderah remain in my memory.
The treasures of the Kings' Tombs had not yet been unearthed,
and in any case belong to decorative rather than to constructive
art. Denderah, being late (and those heads also, perhaps), reflected Greek influence, and doubtless on that account were easier
for me to appreciate. I am not ashamed of liking late styles. They
ought to be the surest expression of human taste, since technique
has been mastered and accidental mannerisms have been overcome; only the volume and seriousness of inspiration may be
wanting, unless the artist is able to transcend and rebuke his
epoch, as the tragedians and Socrates and Plato could do in
Athens. Then we obtain the maturity of lateness with an early
inspiration revived as philosophy or religion.

Of course we went to the Pyramids. The tourist talk and the
tourist foreground dominated; the great question was whether we
should ride or not ride a camel, ascend or not ascend the great
pyramid, pulled up at each step (four feet high) by an acrobatic

Arab: and little grinning English Tommies were crawling over the Sphinx. I said to myself: *Non raggionam di lor, ma guarda e passa.* It was not altogether easy to look. Sand had half buried the base of all these monuments, and we were there pert and self-conscious pygmies, incapable of imagining or understanding what they signified, and playing with their ruins like a child with his rocking-horse. There remained only the vain traveller's satisfaction in saying, yes, I have been there, I have seen the Pyramids; and the fact of having seen them, however flightily, certainly leaves in the psyche a material *point d'appui* for anything we may otherwise learn about them. I have since read two or three books about Egypt, and there have been notorious discoveries, so that nowadays a young girl can't stand still in the street without reproducing the outlines of the ancient Egyptians. This was probably not the immortality for which they cared so much; but I am at a loss to conceive what that immortality could have been. It is not a subject to which anything in me responds. Let the dead, I say, bury their dead; yet those who have no sense for eternity try to prolong their existence by desiccating their bodies or disembodying their souls. It is in either case a sham, ghastly or ghostly. Leaving that, I thank the Egyptians for the standard they have set up for mankind in the solidity of their architecture. We may refine all we like; unless we rival or surpass that solidity, that superhuman permanence, those symbols of silent potentiality and eternal peace, we shall always remain secondary, temporary, capricious, and childish. We shall always be doing things that are partial failures, that we must abandon at once for something different, and that even when they are in fashion disquiet us more than they satisfy.

It was not as a pious pilgrim that I went to Palestine; nothing that I could expect to find there would affect my personal religion or philosophy. I went as a sceptic, to visit the birthplace of religion in others and if possible to understand that religion better. These parched Semitic deserts have been the fountain of inspiration to the whole modern West and to a great part of the East: only pagan antiquity, India, and China have reflected rationally upon the subject, and leaving inspiration to take the forms it likes, have naturalised it in a calm philosophy. Nor was the expression of religion in art, as in Europe and in Egypt, that which I looked for here. Here the chief art was religious eloquence and that can be studied more quietly by one's own fireside. The rest was barbarous and secondary. But the primitive condition of the country—then (1905) still under Turkish rule—the mixture of races, languages, and costumes, the religious feuds, the medley of ruins and shrines, and the petrified deathlike aspect of these ravines and river-beds without water, and these hills without verdure, formed an ominous theme for historical meditation.

I was now alone, having parted from Mrs. Beal at Assouan. She was bound further up the Nile; but with the first cataract, the great dam, and the half-submerged temple of Phylae my journey had come to its proper end. Nubia lay beyond my range: sun, sand and natives were nothing to my purpose. I had made for the Holy Land in the only way then practicable, by sea to Jaffa. The little port, which we entered in a row-boat by scooting on the top of a wave between two rocks, the little town clinging to the face of the cliffs, and the little railway climbing the mountains to Jerusalem, were much to my taste: small, indifferent material things, to be disregarded by souls full of great passions. And the country, not unlike Castile, all rock and moor, also preached frugality, austerity, reserve. It taught the overfed, overdressed child of the West how unnecessary were most of his burdens.

In Jerusalem I was in the hands of a guide assigned to me by Cook's Agency, a short middle-aged native who spoke English and had been converted to Anglicanism from his doubtless Jewish affiliations. He had no sense for the matters historical and artistic, that really interested me, and thought it his duty merely to point out sites and name names, none of which were worth remembering. I stayed three weeks in Jerusalem, waiting for the rain to stop, for I had planned to go by carriage through Samaria and Galilee to Damascus. It would have been a memorable trip; but the roads, people said, would be impassable, and I finally gave up the idea.

So long a stay rather taxed my poor guide's ingenuity to think of new sights to show me; but some of the last were among the best. For instance, he took me one day to a Greek monastery some miles away in the country: the drive was not uninteresting, and the glimpse of the religious life of the Orthodox, and of their persons, was just what I was looking for and seldom found. My guide, while not unknown or turned away, seemed not to be on very good terms with the natives of any persuasion: doubtless they thought him a renegade for not being converted to their own sect. I seemed to be an object of curiosity to these Greek monks, as much as they were to me. Unfortunately, I couldn't say anything to them directly; but we exchanged courtesies through the interpreter. Meantime I observed their aspect and ways. Nothing religious: a sort of childish animality: no trace of Greek features, except in some the very large, thick-lidded eyes. They were all rather small, and of course long-haired and bearded. One couldn't help thinking of Christ, who no doubt in the pictures had been made to look somewhat like them: but to me the assimilation was distinctly unpleasant. Christ should never be painted to look like a savage or like a woman. There should be the dazzling apparition of a god, breaking through an ascetic figure.

Another afternoon, on foot, we went to a Catholic monastery on the Mount of Olives. Here the trouble with my guide didn't matter. An Italian monk showed us the garden; I at once established friendly relations; and he explained to me that the ancient olive tree was not the same that had stood there in Christ's time, but was an offshoot of it; they had planted other offshoots near by, against the time when the present hollow contorted old stem should crumble altogether; and he gave me a few leaves of this, which I sent in a letter to Mercedes. I felt at home: my vocation to live in Italy began to show itself.

We had of course been to Jericho, and the shores of the Dead Sea. Geographically, this was of the highest interest. What a cleft in the crust of the earth, to prove how rotten it is inside! The view across the Dead Sea from the Mount of Olives, with the

mountains of Moab opposite, shows the same cleft in a grander
light: the rottenness is not felt, only the sublimity of the depths
and the heights, the gamut of nature keyed up to that of the
Hebrew prophets.

As to Christian associations, legendary or historical, my own
ignorance and the insensibility of my guide completely smothered
them. I saw everything, but without even a borrowed illusion of
devotion, such as I could have caught easily from a pious Catholic.
Turkish soldiers kept guard at the supposed birthplace of Christ,
lest Christian sects should come to blows over it: and everywhere
ecclesiastical quarrels and modern desecration vulgarised sacred
and poetic things.

Of the Mussulmans I had a better opinion: they were openly
warlike, openly sensual, proud, chivalrous, and capable of friendship. They were poetical and manly, bold and bravely resigned to
the will of God. They didn't overestimate their own importance in
the universe; but they despised a servile mind. All this, however,
was a mere ideal, a fancy of my own: I had no means of verifying
or disproving it. It would have required a youthful and adventurous courage to explore the East like a Doughty or a Charles de
Foucault, and in the first place a sportsman's agility and endurance, with a perfect command of Arabic. I was reduced to catching
glimpses here and there of men and manners, and filling in the
rest with memories of the Arabian Nights. My reading of the
Koran had not awakened me to anything new: the lyric parts were
inferior to the Psalms, and the legends inferior to those in the Old
Testament; whereas to compare with the parables and the maxims
of the New Testament there was absolutely nothing. Ritual sublimity the Koran, in the original, may well possess. Eloquence and
nobleness belong to speech even in Spain, and they have a quality
that is not Roman, but must be Moorish.

As to the Arabian Nights, I had feasted on them recently with
unexpected pleasure. What I had read of them in boyhood had
inspired me with a priggish contempt. I thought the tales (as they
are) chaotic and demoralising, although I read them in a drasti-

cally expurgated translation. But now Mrs. Berenson, who had
charitably received me at Settignano when I was ill with a bad
catarrh, had piled the sixteen volumes of the French version of
Mardrus upon the table by my bedside; and if they didn't cure me,
at least they reconciled me to being laid up. The view of life, like
the life reviewed, is still chaotic; and I can understand the dislike
expressed by pious Moslems at having them regarded as true
pictures of their family life. The pictures belong to the general
tradition of the whole East, India and China included: they are
satirical, summary, realistic, exquisite, and entertaining. The ex-
aggeration, Gargantuan or love-sick, has irony in it; the popular
story-teller indulges our unrestrained dreams, and at the same time
laughs at them. The ribaldry renders all this more piquant and
joyous than it otherwise would be; also less narcotic and vainly
imaginary, because sensuality after all belongs to real life, and
experience can at once justify the interest in it and discount the
illusion. I don't find the Arabian Nights, unexpurgated, demoralising, as I did, expurgated, when I was a boy. I see now that they
are playful and how much they adorn and embroider the commonplaces that they play upon. There is indeed no moralising in them,
nothing by way of a lesson; wisdom and poetry only in scraps,
comedy only in episodes, tragedy hardly at all. Yet we have the
daily texture of life spread before us in its crudity and in its magic;
the experience and the imagination of an unabashed creature that
understands nothing, but meets everything with the strength and
cunning of a man and the impulses of a child.

In Damascus I remembered the judgment that my young friend
Duer Irving had passed on Seville. Seville was nothing unless you
had a horse and a love-affair, and then it was everything. The
horse and the love-affair being out of the question for me at
Damascus, the place threatened to mean nothing to me: yet that
was not altogether the case. The suk was the best I saw in the
East: there was also a most picturesque market or exchange or
caravansary, where merchants and travellers gathered, where the
merchandise was on view, and where the central fountain, under

the open sky, and the surrounding domes and cloisters, produced most wonderful effects of light and shade. Here leisure and business, profit and enchantment, were not divided. The suk was comparatively lofty and wide, like the nave of a church, with much the same effects of light, for it was covered partly by stone arches, partly by wooden roofs, and in places only by awnings, so that patches of sunlight shone out here and there, to dazzle the eye and deepen the grateful shadows of the rest. The ground was earth to be trodden by beasts of burden, led in familiarly without undue regard for pedestrians; and the booths on either side for the most part had no great depth, but displayed all their wares within reach of the hand. One of the booths especially attracted my attention, and as a stubborn client happened one day to be bargaining and making his choice for half an hour, I was able to watch the scene unmolested at a discreet distance. It was a carpet shop. There was a broad counter in front, at one end of which sat the venerable merchant, impassive and apparently indifferent, dressed in black, red, and white, with a long grey beard. Behind him were two rows of rugs rolled up and standing on their edges, like so many barrels. The quality, colours, and pattern of each were sufficiently visible to entice the eye, and provoke at request that the precious thing should be unfolded. Then the youthful assistant would leap up from the other end of the counter, pull the particular carpet down and spread it out over the counter or if need be on the ground outside. This agile young man was beautifully dressed and fit to represent any of the adolescents in the Arabian Nights. He wore a red fez, a white-and-green striped tunic reaching down to the ankles, with tight sleeves, but growing full at the bottom and held together at the waist by an ample sash, that served also for pockets, and was made of a yellow brocaded stuff: and he was shod with yellow babouches. After many rugs, some of them lovely, had been spread out and rolled up again, he had to bring down and extend the heaviest of all, a great red one that covered the whole width of the road; but I didn't stay to see whether the bargain was finally struck. A great camel was coming up the path: he couldn't be allowed to tread on that invaluable carpet, so up it had to come again in the twinkling of an eye; and I took advantage of the excitement to slip away. It is an awkward position for the curious not to wish to buy anything: if they look, the tradesman at once thinks he has a likely customer, and begins to exhibit and praise his wares. You feel like an intruder and have to hurry away. For this reason I have never been able to examine precious objects, even books, except in shop windows.

Of architectural beauties I found little in Damascus; it was at Baalbek, on the way back, that the imagination was stirred, if not with beauty, at least with wonder. The scale and extent of the monuments here rivalled the Egyptian, while the style and the religious inspiration remained Greek. Perhaps of all periods in history the Hellenistic, between Alexander and Caesar, corresponds best to my feeling. In reading Plutarch, who lived later himself, but most of whose heroes lived earlier, I am put out by his doctrinaire morality, as if all men and ages ought to follow the same model; also by the limitations of the older heroes' minds. They were wonderful, they were perfect, but they were slaves to local traditions and special passions. The full-grown human soul should respect all traditions and understand all passions; at the same time it should possess and embody a particular culture, without any unmanly relaxation or mystical neutrality. Justice is one thing, indecision is another, and weak. If you allow all men to live according to their genuine natures, you must assert your own genuine nature and live up to it. Now, with Alexander, a great part of the East in fact, and the whole world in prospect, were introduced into the sphere of the West, into the narrow military life of the ancient city: yet the gods of the city were not abandoned; but exalted into gods of the open rational philosophic mind, they were retained to preside over a universal empire. Heliopolis, the City of the Sun, seemed to me to represent this ideal fusion. It was immense like the East, but unlike the East it was not miscellaneous. The miscellaneous East very soon overwhelmed it, as the miscellaneous North overwhelmed the Western Empire. Yet ruins give ground for hope; for although nothing can last forever, now and then good seasons may return.

On the way from Beirut to Athens, we saw the coasts of Cyprus and Rhodes, and stopped at a small island and then at Samos. In these islands I first trod Hellenic ground, but without emotion: hardly a stone, hardly a head, reminded me of Hellas. Athens itself, for the most part, was uninspiring. I engaged a youngish man, a Cypriot journalist, as a guide and as a teacher of Greek; but in both respects, in my two months at Athens, I gathered little new knowledge. The social foreground was too cosmopolitan, and the material foreground too ugly and insignificant. We went on one excursion, intending to reach Delphi; but at Corinth we found that the steamer had been purloined by a private pleasure-party, and I had to be satisfied with a trip to Nauplia, for Tiryns and Mycenae, and to Epidaurus. This last, my most remote point, proved the most inspiring. Whether it was the light and the solitude, the steepness of the pit, the completeness of the theatre (except for the stage) or the sombre wooded hills above, somehow all the poetry of early Greece seemed to flood the place: small, heroic, silvan, open to sea and sky, lyric and divinely haunted.

In the Acropolis I had two or three unexpected intuitions. One regarded the vitality, the dash, the solidity of Greek architecture. The lion's head at the corner of the immensely projecting cornice in the Parthenon seemed to have all the picturesqueness of a gargoyle: and the entablature was not what its name and usual aspect imply, a wooden beam laid across posts: it was a great wall built up over a foundation of columns, like the wall of the Doge's palace in Venice, firmer if not so high. On the other hand, that bold cornice and those broad pediments lent it an even greater dignity. This effect, of the temple raised over the peristyle, was new to me, and important. It removed the reproach, that pursues buildings of one storey, of lacking weight and height and being set up on stilts, propped up, rather than built. Here the burden carried seemed sufficient to ennoble the bearers, and to justify their stoutness, their number and their fidelity to one model, like hoplites in a phalanx. This architecture was not merely utilitarian and economical; it was religious and martial.

Beautiful beyond words seemed to me the door and the Ionic

porch at the back of the Erechtheum. Byzantine, Saracenic, and
Gothic cannot surpass such a thing in loveliness; their advantage
lies only in allowing greater variety, so that in a larger and more
complex world they could diffuse disparate beauties, more picturesque and romantic than those of Greek buildings.

I left Greece disappointed, not with Greece but with myself.
I should have been young and adventurous, knowing the language
well, both ancient and modern, and travelling alone, with infinite
time before me. Then if the historic Ilyssus proved to be a rub-
bishy ditch in a dusty waste, I could have found another Ilyssus
in some mountain gorge in which to bathe my feet like Socrates
and Phaedrus and pass in dialectical thought from sham rhetoric
to rational love. But the foreground was a dreadful impediment,
and I was the worst of impediments, with my middle-aged ignorance, my academic ties, and my laziness. Hellas must remain for
me an ideal, a thing to recompose, as the Evangelists recomposed
their idea of Jesus, so as to individualise and replenish their ideal
of Christ. The real Greece is dead, pulverised, irrecoverable. There
remain only a few words and a few relics that may serve to suggest
to us a rational ideal of human life.

With this the moral object of my journey was attained, or
shown to be unattainable; but there remained one more scene to
peruse, and I took ship from the Piraeus for Constantinople.
Galata, where the hotels are, was nothing; but I could walk across
the bridge, guided the first time, afterwards alone, to St. Sophia,
the other mosques, and the stray sights of the old city. No exterior
effects at St. Sophia, even from a distance. Remove the picturesque accident of the minarets, and you have a flat dome little
more beautiful than that of the Pantheon in Rome; in character
almost like the Baths of Diocletian. Was this dome intended to be
a marvel externally, like that of the Mosque of Omar? In any case,
it is a marvel internally: as if a tent held down by a dozen pegs
had been lifted by the wind, and crystallised in mid-air. The eye,
as it travels down over the great arches to the arcades of the galleries and aisles, is a little distracted by the oblique lines of the
Mohammedan carpets and pulpit, and the hideous yellow discs

hung high on the walls; but discounting this, and examining things more closely, wonder returns. What columns, what capitals, what walls! Roman luxury refined by Oriental taste, Roman grandeur of scale and mass spiritualised by mystic aspiration. This vast chamber is a sanctuary, regal in magnificence but open to the sky and air; this unity is infinitely rich in detail, this heaven has its hierarchy of dignities and beauties. A theocratic and imperial Church displays its poetry here, as it displays its pride at St. Peter's.

After this, at once surfeited and disappointed, I wanted to see nothing more, suppressed my love of new places, and stopped only to rest at Buda-Pesth and Vienna. I meant to leave Vienna, at least, for another occasion, when I might make a long stay, and see the Catholic, gay, and courtly elements of Germany, so utterly ignored in the view of Germany obtainable from America; but I have never been in Vienna again. In fact, I have never again travelled for the sake of travelling. My orbit has become narrower and narrower, dropping one loop-line after another: somewhat as the ball at the gaming-table runs round in smaller and smaller circles, more and more slowly, hesitates at the edge of each socket and then finally flops down and settles comfortably into the predestined resting-place. And the predestined socket in my case was Rome: *omnium urbis et orbis ecclesiarum,* says the inscription at the Lateran, *mater et caput.* Mother and head of my moral world, surely, and central enough even to-day: balmy also, humanly habitable at all seasons, full of ancient and modern and even of recent beauties, and inhabited by a people that more than any other resembles the civilised ancients. I could not be more at home anywhere, while preserving my essential character of stranger and traveller, with the philosophic freedom that this implies. Thus I renounce travel here, where I may still continually travel in thought to all ages and countries and enjoy the divine privilege of ubiquity without moving from my fated centre of gravity and equilibrium.

# CHAPTER IV

## *ON THE SOUTH DOWNS*

NOT far from Petersfield in Hampshire, just above the village of South Harting, a steep road climbs up the side of the Downs. The valley, as you ascend, begins to look more and more like a map, with its variegated patches of green fields, hedgerows and woods, and an occasional house that seems remarkably neat and toylike in the distance. At the top, the back of the Downs becomes rolling and bare, with rough heather and grass and here and there a copse in the hollows. The sweep of the horizon is unbroken all round, the wind blows fresh and invigorating, and in clear weather the sparkling line of the Channel is visible, and the Isle of Wight. The silence is primeval. Here sheltered in part by some high hedges that enclosed squares of grass as if for tennis courts or gardens, stood a little white pavilion with a flagstaff; the cottage for the man once in charge of the "semaphore" or signal service from London to Portsmouth. That form of communication was now obsolete, although bonfires were still occasionally lighted on the topmost knoll. I don't know by what chance this spot attracted Russell's attention, but it appealed to his love of space and of unchallenged dominion. There was not a house in sight, and a vast stretch of moor and woodland was available for purchase. He bought it, using it at first as a retreat for week-ends and holidays, but eventually enlarged it, put on another storey, a library in a wing, and even a tower, made roads, and turned it into his chief residence.

The natives for some reason had fallen into the habit of calling the place the telegraph house. Russell was not sensitive to the magic of names. He had consented, I suppose at the Scotts' suggestion, to call his ugly villa at Maidenhead *Amberley Cottage,*

Amberley being his second title, by which his father had been known; and now when he had a place of some character and potential beauty he adopted for it that absurd name, *Telegraph House*. Soon, however, in the jolly English way, the absurdity was domesticated, and everybody called the place T.H. It was comfortable, had no pretensions, and yet a magnificent position, a wild and varied domain, and the charm of solitude. I visited it repeatedly during thirty-two years, under its three mistresses, all three of whom I found hospitable and friendly, and of all places it is perhaps the place where I have breathed most freely.

When first Russell took me there, no road existed within the grounds, and the cart that met us at the nearest country station cut deep ruts in the grassy hillside as we wound and tilted, like a boat over the waves, up to the little house. I had expected that we should be alone there, in a sort of bungalow; but at the door we were welcomed by two modest-looking women, evidently mother and daughter, who smiled and spoke not exactly as servants would. Mrs. Turner, for so the mother was called, must be, I thought, a sort of landlady or housekeeper; and then I remembered, on hearing the daughter called Martha, that a Martha Turner had been the secretary at Swinburne and Co., Engineers, where Russell was a partner. When those ladies unhesitatingly sat down at table with us, I began to understand how matters stood. Martha Turner was now his private secretary. He was a married man unable to get a divorce, because Lady Scott, no less proper and more fashionable than Mrs. Turner, chaperoned her daughter everywhere, even to hotels where the young man of the moment occupied the adjoining room. Nevertheless, Russell was engaged to be married to Martha Turner prospectively, in case he should ever be free: and meantime he occupied the room next to hers and her mother's at T.H. To nonplus Mrs. Grundy, his identity was concealed from the servants and from people at the village; Mrs. Turner was the legal tenant, and all letters had to be addressed under cover to her. He was only Martha's young man who came for an occasional visit.

I never disliked Martha Turner. She was a clean honest young woman, reasonable, docile, with a good complexion and a copy-book hand. She was the absolute slave and adorer of her lord and master, and juster to him than his other lady-loves. It must not be supposed that in this case or in that of Emma Billings a promise of marriage was a treacherous means of seduction. There was no need of such a promise. Talk of marriage may have come in, in both cases as a vague ideal; but Martha Turner was honest enough to know that her love-affair was its own reward. The motive force had not been ambition to be a countess: it had been old, simple, irresistible human nature. She loved him truly and was too faithful to rebel at anything. A separation was inevitable. I don't know on what terms they managed it; but he never wholly deserted her as a friend or perhaps even as a lover. There was nothing in him of the poet or the Don Juan, nothing of the gallant, fanciful vola-tile lover. His ideal was the home, or several homes: in a polyg-amous way he was essentially the faithful husband, like Isaac and Jacob, or like Louis the Fourteenth. Had he been an Eastern potentate or a very rich man he might have managed better, keeping all his wives going at once in separate establishments. But in England that was inadmissible. He wanted each wife to be his legal spouse, as did Henry the Eighth; and they too de-manded it. Hence his embarrassments and their tears.

This idyll had a romantic setting, worthy of Rousseau; but the conversation at table was like that in a respectable boarding-house; and Russell was discretion personified, explaining nothing, and leaving me to gather my impressions undisturbed. That was in 1891; I saw and heard nothing of T.H. or Martha Turner for the next two years: but in July, 1894, when for various reasons I was lying low in America, a new chapter opened in this romance. "I was so glad," Russell wrote, "to get your cable and to know that I shall find you in Cambridge. . . . It would be so nice if you would get me lodgings in Cambridge or a room in an hotel— anyway so long as I am near where you are." Why he should so unexpectedly come to America was a mystery: but I knew that he liked long slow sea voyages, and was not surprised that he should choose the *Cephalonia*, the most Bostonian of Boston boats, for the trip. When people cable to you, and suddenly express an affectionate desire to be near where you are, though that place be Cambridge, Massachusetts, in August, it is a sure sign of trouble; and I was rather puzzled on my part how to find a suitable place where Russell might lodge. I was living at my mother's in Roxbury, where we couldn't ask him to stay; no hotel existed in Cambridge and no lodging of the English sort, with a sitting-room and food served separately. I could move, however, to my rooms in the Yard, and put him at the Colonial Club where the restaurant was in working order, and pleasantly deserted. Except for the extreme heat, this arrangement proved pleasant enough. My room was comparatively cool and comfortable, with an outlook on trees and grass, and not much noise, and I took my meals with him at the Club.

One day, when we were at luncheon, in walked William James, with his usual vivacity. "You remember Lord Russell," I explained, "who visited you here eight years ago." "Ah yes. You have put on flesh," James observed with a medical smile, as they shook hands. It was very true; and Russell's loose white flannels, with jacket ridiculously short, did nothing to disguise the fact. Nor was it a comic or jolly fatness. He was already suffering acutely from varicose veins. His air was preoccupied and at the same time a little vacant. He had too many things to think of, and none of them rewarded thought.

The mystery of his journey—he was on his way to California—was solved one day when he took two photographs out of his capacious breast pocket and asked me which of those two women I thought he had better marry. As he was legally married already and not likely to be free for years, the question was speculative, and for my speculative mind easy to answer. I replied at once, "Neither." One was Martha Turner, looking like a particularly tidy policeman or soldier, conscious of being photographed. She had no superfluous hair, or anything else superfluous. Russell said she was a brick, and I readily believed it. But why marry a brick? In the other lady, quite unknown to me, everything on the contrary seemed to be superfluous. Veronica (for I never saw her and that is all I know of her name), Veronica didn't look very young; rather battered, theatrical and unhealthy. No doubt she was appealing, being unhappy, and perhaps intelligent. Russell explained that she belonged to an Irish but prosperous family in San Francisco, had lived long in Europe, was a Catholic and called herself an artist. All this, in 1894, went very well with being at once fashionable and advanced. It was to her, I could see plainly, that Russell's heart inclined for the moment. He suffered at the thought of giving her up, and he might never have had the strength to do it. It was she who thought better of it, and broke off their relations.

That she had been greatly tempted, I can well believe. Imagine a woman of thirty, not particularly beautiful, frail, sensitive, thinking herself highly cultivated and a woman of the world, but idle and homeless: what a divine vocation, to capture a superman, to tame him, to save his soul and to become a British peeress, with a lovely home and a fixed nationality! But she seems to have had a shrewd elder brother who managed her property, and kept an eye on her generally; and I suspect that she also had an experienced confessor. Doubtless they warned her. Anyhow, Russell wrote from San Mateo: "I am thrown back rather than forward . . . and am rather upset again. . . . There will be an issue some day." And some months later from Maidenhead, "Veronica has retired into an inscrutable silence. . . . It was very painful and a blow to one's vanity, that abrupt breaking off: and yet the relief was immense . . . Veronica saved the situation by cutting the knot—what I regret is that fear and pique were the cause of the step. I wish I could attribute it to unselfish consideration of Martha's interests." So I discovered that Veronica had known all about Martha. The lady had been aware that she was being asked to promise to marry a man who not only had a legal wife but had promised to marry somebody else whenever he should be free!

When Russell says that being finally jilted by Veronica was a "great relief," but regrets that her action was not due to "unselfish consideration of Martha's interests" he reveals two sides of his character that afterwards reappeared on various occasions. One was a certain passivity or fatalism in his actions and feelings. He doesn't see the absurdity of asking one rival lady-love to sacrifice herself for the sake of another, while never thinking of making the sacrifice himself and cutting the knot in the beginning. That falling in love is often fatal and involuntary may be granted, although it can sometimes be headed off; but then reason and duty come in, in a strong soul, to suppress or sacrifice the passion. But what is reason or duty? Either another passion—the passion for harmony and integrity in the soul—or social conventions, expediencies and taboos. Against everything of the latter kind a transcendental free spirit rebels: and there I see the secret of tragic strength being often mixed with an extraordinary fatalistic weakness. You are tossed by every wave, and yet something in you observes your plight and fundamentally despises you. Most of the heroes and heroines in Racine suffered from this intellectual elevation in moral helplessness, Phèdre especially;* and if Titus in *Bérénice* masters his passion, he does it behind the scenes under political pressure and against his will, so that his exercise of freedom

---

* J'aime! Ne pense pas qu'en disant que je t'aime,
  Innocente à mes yeux, je m'approuve moimême,
  Ni que du fol amour qui trouble ma raison
  Une lâche complaisance ait nourri le poison.
  Objet infortuné d'une vengeance céleste,
  Je m'abhorre encor plus que tu ne me déteste . . .
  Que dis-je? Cet aveu que je te viens de faire,
  Cet aveu si honteux, le crois-tu volontaire?
  Tremblante pour un fils que je n'osais trahir,
  Je te venais prier de ne le point hair:
  Vains projets d'un coeur trop plein de ce qu'il aime!
  Hélas! je ne t'ai pu parler que de toimême.
  
  Phèdre. Acte II.

seems but another instance of slavery. And it was this complete helplessness that Racine felt to be tragic: he wrote *Bérénice* because he found in Suetonius the phrase: *invitus invitam.* Now in Russell the passion for harmony and integrity was entirely absent: the transcendental spirit, though conscious of itself, had no representative on the stage, nor even a chorus to fill up the interludes; it was silent, and therefore, for the public, nonexistent. He explains this himself in an unusually reflective letter written during this visit to America.

"San Mateo, Cal.
"12 Aug. 1894.

"You will think I have been remiss in not writing to you before to thank you for the lovely time you gave me at Cambridge. It was very peaceful and very restful: just what I wanted . . . I don't think I ever took in your character before so distinctly as I did this time: we are opposed as entirely as possible. You are all for rest in the perfection of form with the negation of an end as either existent or important: I am all for the emotional strife and struggle, however vague and however formless, as being at least a reaching toward some end unknown, and seen only by faith as existing at all. Is not that so?" This he modifies two months later, writing from Paris, October 19th, 1894: "Why do you refer to me as loving strife for its own sake? . . . I desire peace and rest above all things now, I hate to be involved in a personal turmoil which invades and makes impossible a philosophic calm. Of course I may have said, and it is true, that strife does me good, braces me, and brings out my best qualities: but I don't welcome it."

Strife undoubtedly brought out his ability, his cleverness, wit, and gift of satire and invective; they say he was an excellent debater. But that was play-acting: it made him unfair and superficial. He had learned too well from cheap politicians and expensive lawyers to defend his brief and to close his eyes to truth and to justice. Nor does "reaching toward some end unknown, and seen only by faith"—an endless end, or the Eternal Feminine—seem his best side to Platonists like Lionel Johnson and me. His best side in our opinion was his intellectual freedom or transcendental detachment. In the midst of his shabby adventures, which whatever he may have been reaching towards brought him nothing but "expense of spirit in a waste of shame," this heroic spirit remained alive, as in all romantic prodigals; it was proud and brave enough not to be overwhelmed by any folly or any mischance. For this I admired him to the end, as I do Byron, not for what he did or thought, but for what he was.

This time, however, the well-advised Veronica saved him in saving herself, and he made his trip to San Francisco to no purpose. I profited by it in having his company for a week at Cambridge and then receiving various confidential letters and a copy of *Leaves of Grass,* as a memento of his visit. He had been patient in the extreme heat of a Boston August, and had taken pains to be civil; yet he was not at his best in a strange environment. He was not adaptable, and found queer things wrong rather than amusing. In England, where he freely found fault with everything, his satire was intelligent, his misrepresentations witty, and his discomfort feigned. He still felt himself there the cock of the walk, as in his first youth, and that pose became him. At first it was justified enough by his intelligence, his physique, and his title; it was dramatically proper and carried off with great effect, even if destined in the end to become tragic. But now the pose of moral high-mindedness seemed less becoming, as when, for instance, he wrote that he "feared" that Veronica acted from pique and not from "unselfish consideration of Martha's interests." This tone is an echo of his Low Church breeding. When he was in prison for bigamy he composed a book of "Lay Sermons" and published it. Russell was not only an engineer, he was also a member of the bar and had practised for years as an attorney. Applied science naturally figures in the budget of the superman and the enlightened despot: it developed Russell's *virtù*; but applied sophistry, used in the service of any prejudice or passion, narrowed and cheapened his mind. In these "Sermons," he preaches against tradition and legal control, with crushing texts from the Gospels quoted maliciously by an unbeliever. It sounds like cant and hypocrisy; yet Russell was blurting out his sincerest convictions, like any poor man ranting in Hyde Park. Indignant dogmatism was another helpless passion that would invade him before he could stop to look and think: the more tart and feeble his maxims, the prouder he felt in defending them. His brother Bertie had the same satiric gift and the same temperamental fanaticism; but in him perverseness was partly redeemed by historical knowledge and speculative acumen. It seems to me a great pity that their sympathies in politics, as in love, should have been so ill-directed, and that both should wear the crown of martyrdom for such cheap delusions.

To speak of martyrdom is hardly a metaphor. The two brothers were not executed, but both were imprisoned, ostracised, ruined, and driven very largely to waste their talents. At the end some official amends were made to each of them, but too late and only when British standards of propriety had broken down, partly perhaps through their influence. Yet had they found no opposition, I doubt that their fate would have been happier.

That their own independent principles exposed them to singular delusions, quite apart from politics, may be proved in Russell's case by the change of mistress found at T.H. on my next visit there. I first got wind of something new in the realm of Venus when I was asked to "join a house-party" at Amberley Cottage. A house-party in Maidenhead? Who could the woman be? I didn't join the party because that year, 1895, I was but a short time in England; but I did spend a night or two at Amberley Cottage, and at tea one day the lady turned up: "Mollie" I will call her. She was a fat, florid, coarse Irishwoman of forty, with black curls, friendly manners and emotional opinions: a political agitator and a reformer. She took me aside at once and began to lament that Russell should be attached to "that dreadful dull stupid girl," Martha Turner. He must be rescued. I smiled intelligently, but found myself in rather an awkward position, treated at once as a confidential friend, when I had no right to betray Russell's confidence and no wish that he should jump from the frying-pan into the fire, such as this red-cheeked lady's heart would surely be. Nor could I as yet say: "Rescuing him is not for me to attempt: perhaps you might do it." I didn't think he wished to be rescued; and I knew nothing about her except what she had now revealed, which rather suggested that to be rescued from her would be more urgent than to be rescued by her. So I said nothing but discreet commonplaces, and we parted amiably; and amiably we always got on afterwards, during the many years when she was Russell's comfortable wife, and even later, when they had been divorced.

Mollie was a good soul. I think it was a relief to her to give up her politics and "social work"; she retained only a natural motherly kindness to servants and to village children, and to me also, for which I was grateful. She knew what poverty was, and didn't overdo acting the grand lady; remained simple and active, and ready, as it were, to lapse at any moment into her native paddydom without much minding it. She had been an orphan or a foundling, picked up and adopted by a small Irish official or tradesman, who married her later; and she had a grown-up son who bore his name. The old man had died, and now she had two small boys by a second husband, who had brought her to live in London and introduced her to politics and social reform. In those circles she had caught sight of Russell, and Cupid had done the rest.

What could Russell find in this old frump completely to upset him, to make him abandon poor Martha Turner (of whose interests he had been so unselfishly jealous) and to drive him into bigamy, and to a grand trial in the House of Lords, into prison, and into long years of placid married life? Was it intellectual or political sympathy? The absence of antipathy—an antipathy which he would have found in almost any lady—may have helped; but Mollie had no positive intelligence, no real concern about reform; she was simply kind and accustomed to move among social reformers. Could it be sexual attraction? I have not the means of knowing Russell's feelings on this point: he was never ribald or indiscreetly frank in such matters; but the affair with Lady Scott may have been more than an initiation; it may have established an inveterate leaning towards mature charms and motherly indulgence. Anyhow, Mollie's determination to extricate Russell, and his headlong propensity to be re-entangled, overcame every obstacle. She abandoned her two little boys and her husband, who duly divorced her; and she and Russell moved for six months to Reno, Nevada, where he too was divorced, and the two innocents were duly married. The British authorities would not recognise this divorce and remarriage and he was condemned for bigamy by the House of Lords and sentenced to three months in the first division. But this added nothing to his disgrace: on the contrary, it added a touch of antique dignity to his position. His speech in self-defence—duly censored by his lawyers—was excellent, and the only regrettable consequence of having been in prison was the book of Sermons that he wrote there.

What had become of Martha Turner? I was never informed, nor so far as I can remember was I at all curious about it. All those years after 1897 were a somnambulistic period for me, and now seem a blank. But in 1895, she had written me from Newnham, where he had evidently sent her to polish up her education and make her fit to be a countess: very like the Russells to think College a good preparation for wedded happiness! This move, however, had at least left the hermitage of T.H. empty, and ready after 1898 to welcome the blooming bride fresh from Reno, Nevada. For the next fifteen years I periodically found her presiding over that place, attached to it more and more, and as happy as an exacting husband and a dwindling income could allow her to be. She mollified the servants, when Russell had exasperated them; she knew how to control him; she toddled about in her loose tea-gowns with her pack of little white lap-dogs tumbling about her feet, and blinded by the hair in their hidden eyes; and she disappeared for long intervals to her hut or to her tower, for a little solitude, a little nap, or a little effort to rewrite some child's story that some publisher would at last consent to print. She had no religion, but was humble, prudent and resigned. I never heard her sigh as if she regretted her little boys; her troubles seemed to be about the present, about Russell's affairs and expenses. He had become a County Councillor in London, where they had taken a house in Gordon Square, and had card-parties. Bridge and motoring were his most obvious enjoyments and expenses; he took a boyish pleasure in them. He had been the first to apply for a motorist's licence, so that the number of his car was A1.

Sitting by him as he drove was an unmixed pleasure; he did it perfectly, with sureness and ease, and his casual observations, as the road opened up before us and various little scenes appeared, belonged to the original sphere of our friendship. This sphere was play of mind, intellectual light; not philosophy, not theory, but quick intelligence turned upon common things, inquiringly, fearlessly, and universally. Theory and philosophy would have crept in, had we pursued any subject very far; but we never did. I was no more professional at heart than he was, and didn't want to be entrapped by my thoughts. Ours were flying comments, made for the pleasure of making them; a purer pleasure than is to be found in the things on which the comments are made. Speed—never forced speed—and fresh air and the gentle homely charm of the English roads, winding in and out of clean villages, and respectfully skirting any hedged and private domain, made the hours pass gaily and without fatigue: and we had enough sense of things great and distant for these little passing things not to seem too important, and to be judged merrily. We never laughed much, but we were always laughing a little.

Between 1914 and 1919, having been stranded in England by the war, I was often at T.H. I didn't perceive it at the time, but now I suspect that although it was always Russell that wrote to me, it was always his wife, first Mollie and very soon Elizabeth, who really thought of asking me so many times to stay. Their husband was their problem, and they thought I might throw light upon it. Another thing that I then overlooked, and now perceive retrospectively, is that I was no longer young; my presence in itself could not give anybody pleasure; and as to what I might say, or my reputation as a writer, Russell was entirely indifferent. He too was much changed physically for the worse; but in his ways and spirit, at least towards me, he seemed exactly the same; only, being much preoccupied with matters unknown to me, he now had no impulse to unbosom himself as in our younger days. I had lapsed into an old but unimportant acquaintance in his eyes, while in mine he remained the most interesting of mortals. Mollie, being a woman of experience, must have felt this shift in her husband's relations with me, and instinctively made me her confidant, when I was no longer Russell's. The whiskey and water that she drank at meals— and between meals also, I imagine—comforted her a good deal; she wasn't hard to comfort; yet one day she confided to me that she was troubled about Russell. He was in love with somebody else. The truth is I had wondered that this hadn't happened before. More than ten years of contentment with fat old Mollie seemed miraculous. Naturally I couldn't put the matter to Mollie in these terms; but I suggested that Russell was still young, that his temperament was vehement, that he was polygamous without being inconstant, and that it would be wiser to overlook any passing infidelity on his part. They were very happily married and he would return to her.

"No," Mollie said rather gravely, "she wants to be his wife; she wants me to divorce him." Why? Did the silly woman wish to be a countess? No: she wasn't silly, and was a countess already. She was the Countess von Arnim, author of *Elizabeth and Her German Garden*. Russell was very much in love with her.

When I returned to Oxford I procured *Elizabeth and Her German Garden*, asked people about the authoress, and read other books of hers. They were charming, light, witty, showing love of flowers and of solitude, and full of delicate and satirical insight into character, without bitterness or false expectations. In *The Caravaners* she was hard on the Germans: fairer, with greater reason for resentment, in *The Pastor's Wife*. With such horror of domestic tyranny, this extraordinary woman was going to marry Russell! Truly, *la raison n'est pas ce qui règle l'amour.*

I was sorry for Mollie; she had made great sacrifices, almost justified so far by the result. Adaptably she had become attached to T.H. and had helped to render the place more comfortable and homelike. There was a dell of which she was especially fond just below the house: sloping grassy reaches under great trees, with rabbits sitting alert, or galloping away, their white tails bobbing in the air. Here you unexpectedly found deep shade and a sense of being lost and hidden in a green wilderness; while the prevailing notes of that highland solitude were rather openness, buffeting winds, an invitation to adventure, at least in thought, and the freedom of wandering unattached between earth and heaven. Mollie had also attempted a garden, but the site was too exposed, the soil not very rich, and it proved pleasanter to sit indoors, or to stroll through the wilder parts. What folly, after having found a remote refuge and domestic peace with this good woman, and tested the union for so many years, that he should now drive her away, and not only launch upon a new and dangerous voyage, but destroy his home port? As I had been on Martha Turner's side against Mollie, so now I was on Mollie's side against Elizabeth. Russell knew it; of course my external, cynical, Tory view of human affections could make no difference in his conduct; nor did it make any difference in my attachment to him, which had never rested on being pleased with his actions or opinions, but entirely on sympathy with his indomitable person and on admiration of his powers. Naturally we both were silent on the subject of his new love-affair, and events went on without my knowledge. Mollie simply dropped out of the picture. I knew she had been bought off: but this had to be concealed, because English law prohibited divorce by collusion. Divorce might be granted to the injured partner as a release, and as a punishment for the offender: but not if the offender were going to be made happy by it. Such was the wicked fact in this case, at least for the moment; but by some legal machination the divorce was obtained, and Russell and Elizabeth were married. I had no notice of the fact, nor invitation to the wedding, but found her installed at T.H. as a matter of course on my next visit.

By chance, however, I did see Mollie again. I had gone from Oxford to Brighton for a change of scene and air; and walking one afternoon along the Front, I perceived a bevy of little white dogs, like lumps of cotton-wool, moving about the pavement. I looked up, and there was Mollie, richly draped in furs, and rounder than ever. She greeted me amiably, and insisted that I should come up to her lodgings, which she had taken with friends for a week or two. Luckily I never played bridge, or cards of any sort: otherwise I should have found it impossible to avoid taking a hand. There were card-tables, glasses and bottles, and four or five men and women of easy-going manners. I escaped; and to clear my conscience wrote that same evening to Russell, relating briefly but accurately just what had happened. Nevertheless, it seems he was displeased. I suppose I ought not to have gone to Brighton, or ought not to have seen those little white dogs. He could not have expected me not to have recognised Mollie, who had been my very friendly hostess at his house for so many years. For my own part, I was rather glad to have come upon her and found her looking so well and so much in her element. Was she perhaps happier? No: her pride had been wounded; yet it was not the first wound; and now she was free, with a fixed income, and could grow old in peace. She could keep warm and comfortable, while mad wars raged in the world, with her lap-dogs, her cronies, her game of cards and her tipple.

When eventually one afternoon I arrived at Petersfield, on my next visit to T.H., and looked about for the car, I could see it nowhere. After waiting a moment, when the traps that had been there were gone, I asked the guard. No: he hadn't seen Lord Russell's car. "Yes," said another man; "that's it over there, with Lady Russell." Then I noticed a small grey motor, with what seemed to be a young girl at the wheel. I was accustomed enough to being a traveller and a foreigner everywhere not to doubt anything because it seemed odd; and as I ran up to the fair stranger, she waved to me. We had never before set eyes on each other. Russell had written as usual, without saying a word about her, yet here she was alone to meet me. Even at close quarters in the open air she seemed very young: a little thing with a little nose, little eyes, and a little innocent mouth. Yet she had three grown-up daughters and a son of fifteen at Eton. I got in, my things were placed somewhere behind, and we started. She explained at once that she wanted to speak to me before I saw Russell: yet I found that she had nothing in particular to tell me. Evidently it was only that she wished to conciliate me, and thought it would be easier in a *tête-à-tête*. And the reason for this manoeuvre, that seemed unnecessary, was a letter I had written to Russell, which he had shown her, when I first learned that he was divorcing Mollie and marrying somebody else. He ought not to have been displeased with that letter, in which I compared him with Henry the Eighth and with Goethe. Like Henry the Eighth he desired to *marry* all his lady-loves; but that only made him wish later to cut their heads off, that each might make room for the next. Goethe, less bigoted morally and calmer, had finally married only one, the humblest, of his women, who had been his mistress and housekeeper for years. Russell then found himself married in the same sensible way as Goethe. Mollie was used to all his ways, and kept his house economically and in good order. What a mistake to send her away and insist on marrying Frau von Stein! That he *loved* Elizabeth, Gräfin von Arnim, I could well believe; also that she loved him: but why marry? She was a widow, a novelist, and a freethinker. Surely she might accept him for a lover. But if she put herself in his power legally, there would be trouble. With his fixed habits, it would be difficult for a lady to live with him long.

All this was not put so clearly in my letter, but could be read between the lines; and it evidently caused some stir and possibly some alarm in their breasts. Russell protested in a perfunctory way, as a lover and as a Christian, which he thought he was; and

I knew only long after that she had seen the letter at all, when she admitted the profound truth of it. At first, however, she wished to demonstrate—and I was a sort of dummy audience to convince in lieu of the world and of her own conscience—that she was the first *decent* woman to take Russell in hand, and that she had character, intellect, charm, beauty, and sufficient youth to hold him permanently and make a new man of him; or rather, to make him himself again, because his associations, ever since he fell into Lady Scott's hands at the age of twenty-three, had smothered and degraded his true nature. Clever and experienced as she was, she felt that this would appeal to me; that I also *believed* in Russell, against all apparent evidence; and that I should retract the horrid immoral suggestions of my letter, and admit that she was the providential Frau von Stein destined to lift her happier Goethe into a great statesman and a man of the world.

And in spite of the fatal issue, there were elements of truth in her prognostications. She did hold his affections; he spoke of the "anguish" he suffered when she deserted him; protested that he still "loved and worshipped her," that his life was blighted, and that all had been wanton cruelty on her part, because she was incapable of loving anybody, even her own children. These reproaches were absurd; Elizabeth was a cool but tender person; they merely proved how much he was upset and exasperated by losing her. It was also true that he was worth saving: and a certain side of his real gifts actually came to public notice at the end, not especially under her influence, but in politics. Yet, as he knew and admitted, those external occupations didn't touch his heart; they were parts of Maya, traditional whirlpools in which birth plunges us, such as making money, making war, or making love. They compel us to care intensely, as in a dream, for things of no ultimate consequence: and this not merely because those things are transitory, but because the effects of our efforts are incalculable in the end, and we may be bringing about results that, could we foresee them, would appall us. I think that this conviction, perhaps unconsciously, encouraged Russell to let himself go and to plunge into irrational ventures. In him, however, these courses left their mark and became automatisms, soon impossible to withstand or to correct. Maya might be an illusion, but she held him tight.

The marvel was that so many women, by no means fools, thought they could manage him, and that each in her turn believed herself predestined to redeem him and anchor him in the safe haven of her arms. Martha Turner thought so, Lady Scott thought so, Mollie thought so, and now Elizabeth thought so: the simplest, the most battered, the most intelligent of women were alike in their infatuation and blindness. I suppose their vanity conspired with his persuasiveness to deceive them; and he was persuasive: very different as a lover, Elizabeth said, from what he was as a husband.

That his society was charming, his personality dominant, that there was nobody in whose good graces one would rather be, I knew by my own experience. But in friendship liability is limited; each preserves his privacy and freedom, and there is no occasion for jealousy or tyranny. Towards his women, once they were enveigled into an unlimited partnership, Russell was a tyrant. He imposed on them an infinity of petty habits and rules, with the gravity of a strict moralist, and laid down heavily the most puerile and hackneyed saws of politics and conduct as if self-evident. To me these absurdities were amusing and harmless. I knew them by heart; they were parts of his imperious personality, which I accepted merrily when I was with him. He never dreamt that I should accept them for myself. He left me abundantly alone: I was a *hors d'oeuvre* in his menu; so much so that he was genuinely puzzled when in the last years I wrote him that he had been very important in my life. Certainly he had had no influence on my career; but my career was not my life. Mine has been a life of reflection, which he couldn't understand; and he had given me much to think of, many pleasures and many lights. But his wives and his cats were his prisoners, condemned to be petted at pleasure. They had only secret hours for being fondled, and were

treated in public, and ordinarily in private, with a virtuous austerity. His ways of making love were said to be somewhat capricious and exacting: Elizabeth once called them sadistic. And
love-making for him was no laughing matter, no playfulness of a
mad moment. It was a loving wife's sworn duty to be obedient;
and if she rebelled and fled from her husband, he said she was
cruel.

Elizabeth in the beginning was simply the amiable hostess:
always prettily dressed, witty, full of little amusing anecdotes
about her life in Germany. She would walk with me in the dell,
and show me her knowledge of flowers and discriminating love
of them. It was only gradually that she became confidential. She
had money and furniture of her own—not much, as I suppose the
war had cut off whatever her first husband may have left her,
but enough for her to be somewhat independent; and with her
love of solitude, she had found it necessary to set up a bungalow
of her own, where no one was allowed to disturb her. It was a
spacious apartment, charmingly furnished with books, flowers,
and gaily coloured chintz. Here she retired to rest and work. This
was the first symptom of domestic division that came to my notice;
but ultimately she began frankly to confess the difficulties she
found in living with Russell. What they were in essence she made
public afterwards in her novel *Vera*. As she said to me, she began
by making the man in it quite unlike Russell: but as the theme
was her own domestic tragedy, he became more and more like
Russell as the story developed. It is not a good portrait because the
fundamental structure is wrong, if it were meant to represent
Russell; but many of the details are photographic: and I think it
may truly be called cruel to publish them during his life-time.
But he had driven her to desperation; and she developed the spite
of a hunted animal.

For me the scene closes on T.H. rather distressingly, as on
an interrupted performance. The place was materially much im-
proved, the grounds developed, the hall panelled, the rooms fresh-
ened up and adorned; but Russell was preoccupied and silent,

Elizabeth hardly visible save at table, and a mysterious emptiness seemed to pervade the place where, in good Mollie's day, I had felt so free and happy. After the rupture, Elizabeth and I remained, or rather became, very good friends. She occasionally came to Italy; finally she took a house on the French Riviera where at last, she said, she had a garden after her own heart. But no garden can be paradise when all within is a desert. She was desolate and bitter in her old age, and pronounced life to be "a very bad joke."

It was there that she heard of Russell's death, which occurred at Marseilles, not very far from her: for he too had come to the Riviera for a little rest. One of his relations one day turned up at her place, and Elizabeth on recognising the approaching lady, waved a welcome to her, but noticed a strange solemnity in her manner. "Why are you so serious?" she asked. "Frank!" the lady gasped tragically. "What is *he* up to now?" Elizabeth inquired without emotion. "Dead and cremated!" cried the other: and closed the chapter of that love affair sardonically, in sympathy with its theme. For it had been, for both, a false and hollow revival of youth in old age.

After Elizabeth deserted it, T.H. passed for me, and I think for Russell also, into a sort of penumbra. I was living abroad and visited it only once again, in 1923.* At the time of my last trip to England, nine years later, Russell was already dead, and had bequeathed the place to his brother Bertie. Then it underwent a curious transformation. Bertie was temporarily married to his second wife, who had been a teacher at Girton: they had young children and advanced ideas on education. Wasn't T.H. an ideal oasis for an unimpeded experiment in liberty? They would turn the house into a school where children should do exactly as they liked until they found it unpleasant and should learn only what they felt like learning. I don't know what were the results; perhaps the experiment was interrupted prematurely; for before long Bertie and his wife were divorced and the school

* Cf. *Farewell to England*, towards the end of this book.

was merged and lost in that universal experiment in education which nature has always been making just on Bertie and Dora's simple and cruel principles. I have not heard, and hardly wish to hear, what has become of T.H. For me it belongs to the happy past, rescued by being past from being ever changed.

# CHAPTER V

## *OXFORD FRIENDS*

MY FIRST acquaintance with Oxford is recorded in the early chapter on Russell; it was memorable but ended in a blind alley. Russell himself I never saw there, nor had he any affection or respect for that place; and Lionel Johnson and the others who had been his Oxford friends soon vanished into the outer wilderness. My other visits there, except in 1896–7 and after 1911, necessarily fell in the long vacation, since during the working terms I was in America. The colleges were deserted and only married Dons, caged like canaries in suburban villas, could be expected to be in residence. It was my Oxford, therefore, that I first learned to know, not that of the Oxonians.

There was, however, Louis Dyer, my old professor of Greek at Harvard, who lived in Banbury Road, and through him I made the most useful and faithful of my Oxford friends. Like Dyer, he was a Balliol man but not a Don, and they sometimes met at dinner on feast days at the High Table. There I first saw him: a monkey-like creature with a pasty round face, fringed on all sides by patches of black hair; for some disease made it difficult for him either to shave properly or to grow a decent beard. He was a little man, unobtrusive yet always watching everything with a critical experienced eye. In summer he wore a short alpaca coat and grey trousers, and a little cloth hat with a limp brim curling up all round. His shirt was starched, with a corresponding evening waistcoat that left it uncovered; and often the one black stud, expected to keep the two halves together, would slip out and let them fly apart, revealing a hairy chest immediately beneath. With this he sported a very low turned-down collar, and a drooping black evening tie. At a distance he could be recognised by his meditative way of walking, with occasional stops at a crossing or at a shop window; for he lived to observe. His hands were habitually crossed behind his back, and trailed a loose umbrella. Everybody called him "Old Higgs."

Higgs was a private tutor in modern history. In his younger days, when asthma didn't keep him at home, he had travelled a great deal, often on foot, especially through the Baltic countries, and had a rich collection of photographs showing the picturesque aspects of the North. I liked his conversation; for without talking shop or showing any political bias or academic jealousies, he was full of curious information and credible gossip about men and events, recent and remote; and like the learned men of other times, he knew the identity of human nature in all ages, and felt no contempt for manners or ideas that have now gone out of fashion. His standards were those not of a pedant or of a reformer, but of a man of taste. His taste and his diction were thoroughly Oxonian and not more limited or local than anything has to be that is definite; they were pleasant to come upon and to profit by, not as models to be copied elsewhere but as attainments to be prized where they belonged.

Yet his great service to me was of another kind. He showed me all the possible walks about Oxford; after going over each of them two or three times under his guidance, I was able when alone to recognise every turning and every stile, where there was a right of way through a field; and he encouraged me to go rather further than I should have ventured alone, to Islip, for instance, or to Abingdon. His antiquarian lore helped to make the way seem shorter and the sights more individual; and when the distance was too great for a comfortable day's walk, I learned the possible ways of shortening it by taking a train or 'bus to some intermediate point. This Higgs wouldn't do, for economy; and tea also sometimes became a difficulty, because he didn't like to pay more than sixpence for it. Afterwards, during the war, when I started out in the morning, this experience, together with an ordnance-survey map, very much lengthened the radius of my excursions, and I could easily go to Radley and to Nuneham, or to Stanton Harcourt without fatigue. Tea, in winter, would be at a shop in Oxford on my return; but at any inn in the country I could have bread and cheese, with beer, for luncheon: eggs or cold meat the good people never could supply. Old Higgs's days were then over, yet invisibly he often guided my steps; and I may say that I have never seen so many lovely views as through his eyes, because he would not only point them out to me in the first instance, but would find some just epithet to describe them. These modest landscapes rather require a poet to appreciate them; the tourist and even the painter might think them commonplace; their delicacy is aerial, moral, and fugitive, and a happy phrase arrests them best.

I almost saw poor Higgs die. I have called his trouble asthma, but there was a complication of troubles; and while he looked much as usual—that is, very queer—I was startled one day, when strolling with him in the Cornmarket, to have him suddenly stop and stand still, like Socrates struck by epilepsy or by inspiration. He half recovered after a moment and made at once for his lodgings, which were near by, in the first house to the left in Market-Street: pleasant lodgings, sunny with a glimpse of town life from the corner windows, by which he sat and kept the fire going day and night all the year round. I never saw him after that day. A poor devil, no doubt: but I am sure I might easily have led a life like his, had I been less lucky and more studious; and I shouldn't have been unhappy. Unattached academic obscurity is rather a blessed condition, when it doesn't breed pedantry, envy, or ill-nature.

Of notabilities (for which in general I have no liking) the most distiguished who was my friend in Oxford was Robert Bridges. Our friendship began late and was entirely his doing. A friend of his, at the turn of the century, had shown him a copy of my *Interpretations of Poetry and Religion,* saying, "Here is somebody whose philosophy seems to be much like yours. Perhaps you might care to look into him." And in fact I received in America a very kind and appreciative letter on the subject. Still, I never looked Bridges up when I was in Oxford. He was Poet Laureate, I hadn't read him, and I prefer to remain free and perfectly unknown in the places where I am happy. Higgs was not a commitment; but a Poet Laureate . . .

However, when I was caught in England by the war and settled down in Oxford, I somewhere came across him, probably at Corpus. He was an imposing person, twenty years older than I, tall, a little too thin and spare for Olympian Zeus, but otherwise of the same noble and leonine aspect. His manners, however, and his conversation were of the most unpretending, easy, and charming kind, those of the simple, affable English gentleman who remains always young. Soon I began to go sometimes to Chilswell for my walk. Mrs. Bridges proved no less friendly than her husband. I suspect that she, too, had read something of mine and, dear lady, had thought it edifying. Fortunately the religion of that household was not controversial, and until the very end I succeeded in giving them no offence. With her, moreover, I had another point in my favour. When their only son, Edward, came back wounded from the war, I liked him very much, and felt at once, as I told them, as if I had known him all my life. Youth and experience together make a charming combination: the youthfulness secures plasticity, and the experience gives a ground to build upon securely.

Yet in some things my lack of discipline betrayed itself; I hadn't been brought up in an English nursery and an English Public School, nor served in any war. Once, only once, they asked me to spend the week-end at Chilswell. All went well until Sunday morning, when in order to be ready for breakfast downstairs I had to get up rather early. I opened my door, and there were my boots, but no hot water. No mention had been made of any bathroom, and not knowing what to do, I rang, and waited a moment with the door half open. Then I heard an agitated voice saying "He has rung!" Feeling guilty, I closed my door again. Presently there was a knock, and I said perfunctorily, "Come in," thinking it was the housemaid, recalled to her neglected duties. But no, no one came in, and I went to open the door myself. There stood Mrs. Bridges, ghostlike, and without her front hair. She gasped: "What is the matter?" "Nothing, nothing, I only rang to ask the maid for some hot water." "Hot water!" cried Mrs. Bridges, as if shocked. "Only a little, just for shaving," I said apologetically, realising that tubs were not in order, at least not lukewarm tubs. "The maids have gone to church," Mrs. Bridges explained more calmly. "I'll see if I can get you a little." I was really very sorry, and ashamed of myself: I ought to have brought my hot water with me in a thermos bottle, since I was such a sybarite as to require it; but never before in England had hot water not appeared of itself in the morning, wherever I had lodged, and before dinner also, wherever I was a guest. Abashed, I now accepted a small white china jug of hot water from my hostess's hand, and did the best I could with it, a hard beard, a tender skin, and not too sharp a razor. The blessed days of Gillette and of shaving creams had not dawned, and like Olympian Zeus, I should have let nature take her course and possessed a rich and curly beard. Yet Apollo, Hermes, and even Edward Bridges shaved, and also Mars, who needn't have been so young. It would be hard to go back to nature without going back to savagery. That priests and monks should shave, even their crowns, is no doubt a matter of hygiene and cleanliness in warm countries; perhaps, also, as in the case of a nun's hair, a surrender to personal emphasis and boasts. My own instinct would choose hairlessness, long straight robes, and hands hidden in one's sleeves: such an aspect standardises one's personality in the world, and concentrates and purifies it in oneself.

On quite another occasion Bridges, who was a medical man, inveighed against the use of hot water. So bad for the nails and for the hair! With his magnificent *chevelure* contrasting with my baldness, I was reduced to bashful silence in regard to hair; and I kept it also in regard to nails, although not without casting a furtive glance at his hands. They were large, thin, strong hands, that had been used for doing miscellaneous things, and were not dirty: but they hadn't the nursery-maid's pink cleanliness produced by soap and hot water. The nails were grey and thick, like talons. Admirable, no doubt, for certain purposes; but in ages when hot water is available for the toilet, delving is no longer done with the claws, and even jealous ladies do not attempt to scratch each other's eyes out. This does not prove, I admit, that hot water is not a luxury, and unheroic. Even cold water is abhorrent, for external use, to lions and eagles. I admired Bridges' Spartan ablutions, but prefer in this respect to remain a Sybarite. Different animals and different nations cannot be models for one another.

Pleasant as Chilswell was, it was not Bridges at home that showed the grounds of his interest in me. It was Bridges afloat in Oxford. He would often come into the town in the morning; sometimes he was detained, or had business of some kind to do in the afternoon; and, then, knowing my habits, he would come to my lodgings in Beaumont Street at about half-past twelve, when I was finishing dressing, and go with me to lunch at *The George*. Conviviality, for me, has been a great discoverer and cementer of affinities, or at least a substitute for them. Luncheon at *The George* was better than, under the stress of rations, it was likely to be at home; and we habitually enlivened it with a bottle of good burgundy. On these occasions Bridges became again a young man. He had been long a bachelor; he had once spent a whole season in Rome, delighted with riding about the campagna, and no doubt composing verses; whereas when in later life he returned to Rome, everything disgusted him, especially the churches. All that to the free traveller had seemed romantic seemed now to the elderly Anglican false and dead. He could not bear the contrast with the English landscape and with English religious music and sentiment. So, reverting with me, even in familiar Oxford, to the atmosphere of the wandering student and poet, he relaxed his acquired habits of mind. It was for mocking English prejudices, while adoring England, that he valued my writings; and though we seldom or never discussed our respective works, I knew that it was this liberating outlook, partly in the Catholic and partly in the naturalistic direction, that he cared for in me.

That he was influenced by my philosophy is not admissible. A thinker is seldom influenced by another much younger than himself, and Bridges besides did not *understand* my philosophy. His own position was not clear to me until, with reference to his *Testament of Beauty,* he asked me expressly to criticise it and then replied, in a long letter, to my criticisms. He agreed with me, or rather with Kant, as to the *necessarily original* form of the mind, in sensation no less than in religion; but he clung to the belief that this inevitable originality was inspired, and revealed a sympathetic moral spirit in nature at large. Now, my position excludes this belief; because morality and spirit, in my view, express specific and contrary vital interests, as in politics. To assert that one such political or vital interest, say the Jewish or the Anglo-Saxon, coincides with the total inspiration of the universe, is egotism *in excelsis,* and a plain illusion of animal vanity and egotism. Banish that illusion: the vital and political interest concerned remains standing, but only as one local and temporary movement of animal life on earth. It is its own excuse for being, but it leaves the speculative spirit free to transcend it and to admit equally, in their places, all the other vital and political interests that may arise. I would relax English prejudices in the Catholic and in the naturalistic direction by a single and consistent insight, not by casual contrary sympathies. Catholicism is paganism spiritualised: it is fundamentally naturalistic; and the transcendental spirit and the wise statesman may accept Catholicism, where it naturally arises, as a good poetic symbol for the forces and the issues of human life in that phase; not, however, as a scientific revelation of reality or a history of literal facts. Religion is valid poetry infused into common life. It is not a revelation truer than perception or than science. Nature, where it breeds life, is undoubtedly animated by a spirit kindred to man's and to human morality; hence the dramatic sympathy in us with all real or imagined vitality in the universe. Yet this sympathy should chasten rather than inflate us, because it reveals to us how accidental are the objects of our love.

At Christ Church, about 1895, there was a young American whose name I have forgotten, but whom I had known slightly at Harvard. He was pale, quiet, very well dressed, evidently rich but also aesthetic. He seemed always to have a bunch of violets in his buttonhole. It was not surprising that he should have found his way to Oxford, and in particular to Christ Church. There he had spacious but singularly placed rooms that had been occupied by Lord Roseberry. They were in the cellar, immediately to the left as you come through Canterbury Gate, with the windows in pits so far below the level of the pavement that they had large iron cages to protect them. On the other side, however, towards the garden and the meadows, the ground was lower, and there was sunshine and even, through the shrubbery, the suggestion of a view. I found myself there at a large luncheon with sporting youths most of whom I never saw again; I suspect they were all members of the Bullingdon Club. At least this was the case with the very blond modest young man who sat next to me and whom I might also have forgotten had he not taken the trouble to follow up our acquaintance. His name was Harold Fletcher. I had spoken of Oxford architecture, especially of the churches, defending the intrusion of the baroque amid the gothic, as in the lovely porch of St. Mary's. This, although I didn't say anything about religion, was also a defence of Catholic sentiment and practice, and happened to strike in Fletcher a sympathetic chord. This I discovered long afterwards, for he was as silent as he was sensitive; at the moment he only asked me if I should like to drive some morning to Dorchester and see the church there, which was an interesting one.

We started at the appointed time, with the best of weather, in a smart dog-cart, but came to a stop a little beyond Folly Bridge, I wondered why. It was only, Fletcher said, that they were not allowed to drive a tandem through the town, and the groom had to bring the leader down here, to be added on as an afterthought.

Unexpectedly for me, the drive now acquired a picturesque interest of its own, apart from the landscape and whatever was to be seen in Dorchester. It became a festive occasion. Fletcher drove as quietly and as modestly as he spoke, and as much to the purpose, for he seemed perfect master of his horses and of himself. I have always liked to put myself in the hands of skilful people, especially when I am absolutely ignorant of their art. That is a part of my confident faith in nature. Nature may be trusted to do her job even in living creatures, when they are clean-cut and docile, like Fletcher and his two beautiful horses. I afterwards learned, however, that driving with Fletcher was not without its risks, as trusting to nature is also. He was extremely near-sighted, and the story went that one day, when the leader in his tandem had turned completely round, he had gone on driving merrily with the wheeler in the opposite direction. But in my time he wore glasses, and never had the least accident.

When he had left the university and come into his money, being an orphan and much attached to Oxford, he bought the stables in Holywell Street and set up in the coaching business. More than once I had the honour of sitting on the box with him in the coach to Woodstock and Blenheim, and admiring his skill and precision as a whip. Those were public occasions, imposing on him a professional gravity, like that of a captain at sea. Jollier and freer was a trip that his brother and I made with him driving a newly bought four-in-hand, from Leicester to Oxford, fifty miles in one day. It was a lovely trip, taken leisurely, with a long halt for luncheon and rest. We drove into Oxford at a steady slow trot; and at the end, after inspecting the horses minutely, Fletcher came radiant out of the stable. "By Jove," he said, "fifty miles, and never turned a hair!"

So pleasant were these outings that I went with him—though this had to be by train—to the cattle fair at Bicister, and enjoyed the scene greatly, while he did his business. The English air and the English country, apart from mankind, were enough to satisfy me: but here I was entertained also by the country types and the show animals; and there is always a convivial side to such excursions, that brings us back to our chosen friends, to a roast joint and a gooseberry tart and a great mug of ale or of porter.

A simple horsey chap, Harold Fletcher, and ten years younger than I: how much out of my line! Yet everything in this world has an explanation, and there was another side to my friend; something that I should not have required in him, yet without it he would never have been so attentive to me. He was religious: he felt the presence of the invisible. Not that he spoke of such things, for he was sensitive and reserved, but a caricature of his feelings appeared openly in his brother, in many ways his opposite and yet of the same blood. The brother was short and dark, quick and voluble, wished to be an actor, and believed in second sight and in haunted places. He lived in London and knew the personages and gossip of Bohemia. In Harold the taste for the supernatural took the nobler form of an orthodoxy edifying and well-ordered. This feeling, held in reserve, gave a moral background to his ways and to his tastes, even about horses. Horses were made by God; if we saw them from that point of view, we should understand them. That is just what I felt about young men like Fletcher; they are to be approached from within, by way of their genesis and vital impulses, and not to be judged by their utility to other people. Nothing living is a means: all is automatic, spontaneous, justified by whatever it tends to and loves.

I began to see what Fletcher cared for on that first excursion to Dorchester. After visiting the Roman Camp, about which his knowledge was perfunctory (or at least seemed so to me, with my avidity for the setting of ancient life in all its details), we went to see the church, large and perpendicular. In one place a frescoed wall had been recently uncovered. To me it was not very clearly visible or specially interesting, a pastel imitation of stained glass, confused without being brilliant, but what could be made out of the figures sufficed to show the style and spirit of a religious art: quaintly realistic, naïve, and devout. This was evidently what interested Fletcher. His taste had worked back behind the Renais-

sance, to the sentiment of the Middle Ages, to the familiar supernatural, to Catholic piety. There was no pre-Raphaelite affectation in him: he was looking beyond boastful material realism and
theatricality to homely truth, to humble devotion, to revelations in
solitude and comfort in hardship. He was no collector or picture-
dealer; it was not the old clothes of mediaevalism that interested
him but the faith that had worn them.

Fletcher was indeed a devoted friend, perhaps a disciple or
penitent, of Father Waggett's. He asked me expressly to meet
Father Waggett at tea in his rooms; I found a most engaging
clergyman, still young, with no clerical absurdities or insolence,
but with the manners of the world and yet a frank expression of
his apostolic vocation. I was reminded of my *tio Nicolás,* the
Canon of Tarragona; only that Waggett was much younger and
less indolent. I think he may have seen my *Interpretations of
Poetry and Religion,* then recently published; for this was some
years after I had made Fletcher's acquaintance, and not the source
of it. Waggett talked of religion freely and familiarly, like a
Catholic; but it appeared that he was also a naturalist, a zoölogist,
and was writing something that Fletcher had already seen and
admired—I think concerning the instincts of birds. When I expressed a desire to see it, Waggett said he would be glad to come
the next day to Fletcher's again, and read it to me, for it was not
yet printed. I was delighted; but when next day came, I found
Fletcher alone. Father Waggett had sent word that he was very
sorry, but wasn't able to come. "Do you know," Fletcher observed,
"what has probably happened? Waggett, last night, in making his
examination of conscience, asked himself why he was coming here
to read that paper. Was it in the hope of converting you or making
you realise how compatible religion is with science? No: it was in
order to hear himself praised. He mustn't come."

Pleasant to see how shrewd the simple Fletcher could be in
spiritual matters. He was no fool in anything. Our friendship took
root, as if it had been an old family friendship; for instance he
and his brother, who were orphans, took me for a week-end to

visit a maiden aunt of theirs, Lady Mary Marsham, the sweetest
of perfectly deaf old ladies in the neatest of country houses. I have
seldom been happier than with these unexpected friends.

One Sunday Father Waggett invited Fletcher and me to the
midday dinner at Cowley. The refectory was imposing: plain high
white walls, with only a large crucifix over the Abbot's chair, and
a long narrow table, with a white table-cloth, running to right and
left of him along three sides of the room. The monks all sat with
their backs to the wall, leaving the inside of the square empty,
as in the pictures of the Last Supper; only two chairs, like that
sometimes assigned to Judas, were placed inside, for Fletcher and
me. Waggett, in this setting, was absolutely at his ease and like
himself elsewhere. Had we been at a military mess or at a duchess's
table, he would have been the same.

As I found in a conversation we had afterwards in the garden
about immortality, he was an *original*: I mean, that he drew his
convictions from his own inspiration, even when they were, in
words, perfectly conventional. Immortality was presumable and
according to nature, because spirit, the witness, is essentially independent of any world it may discover, prior to it, and in no
way held down to that particular world. Admirable, I thought, if
only he had brought in his natural history at this point, to explain the inevitably transcendental character of perception or
thought, not because thought is existentially independent of animal life, but precisely because animal life, in interaction with its
environment, has imposed such thought. Now this *originality* in
Waggett's sentiments, rendered him a perfect man of the world,
not to be put out or embarrassed by the oddity of his surroundings: he was ready for anything, because what was active in
himself, spirit, could survive anything unscathed, even death.
This is the transcendental principle of courage and of simplicity.
It enabled him to put up, I suppose, with the extreme artificiality,
self-consciousness, and affectation of everybody else in that monastery.

If I described all the poses and movements of those poor monks,

especially of the young ones, it would be thought a gross caricature. Even to me now it seems incredible that I actually should
have seen the idiotic manners that I saw; may I not have dreamt
the whole thing afterwards? Yet there was pathos in those absurdities, because these souls, in need of religion, were groping
for expression and for support in an age and in a Church that had
subordinated religion to national pride and to worldliness. They
had to rediscover or to imitate a cultus: but for discovery they had
no genius and for imitation no taste and no innocence. They therefore seemed fools or hypocrites, when they were sincerely groping
after spiritual rebirth. Not all, perhaps; because in the revival
of Catholicism in England, both Anglican and Roman, there was
also a silly aesthetic sensual side, all vanity and pose and ritualis-
tic pedantry, as in Frederick Rolfe; and this may have contributed
something to the affectations of the Cowley monastery.

Father Waggett some years later went to America and lectured,
I believe, at the Episcopal Theological Seminary at Cambridge. I
went to hear him preach there one afternoon, but I was disappointed. He wasn't the man who, in the garden at Cowley, had
talked about immortality. He was commonplace, cautious, dry.
What wonder, when he found himself bound by politic ties to
people utterly alien to his insights and offensive to his tastes?

The last time I was in Oxford, in 1923, I saw Fletcher's name,
half washed out by the rain, still legible on the gates of the
stables in Holywell, which looked closed and abandoned. Very
likely his enterprise was not successful; such ventures seldom are,
and by that time the motor had dethroned the horse. But Fletcher
had also become a local politician and agent for the Conservative
Party; and seemed, when I last saw him, very pleasantly settled,
with his sister, at Wolvercott. I sent them a large brass knocker
for their new house; and saw it later, brightly burnished, deco-
rating the door that led from the road to their walled garden. I
was leaving England, and didn't knock; but I hope that good
fortune and happiness have done so, and have found their way in.

During the war Oxford was not deserted even by the young:

there was a remnant of boys under military age with others returning wounded or unfit for service, not to speak of a host of
privates become cadets and studying to pass examinations for a
commission. Somehow, I don't remember how, I made the acquaintance of two sets of undergraduates, one at Balliol and one
at Magdalen. Three of the Balliol men remain in my memory, and
one at least has become a celebrity: Aldous Huxley. He was then
apparently almost blind, with a great shock of curly black hair,
and I had no occasion to talk with him. Later, I saw him again,
already a popular novelist, with his wife and child at Cortina; but
I think there was a latent antipathy in our natures and affections
which prevented any spontaneous intercourse. More interesting at
the time was Grattan Esmonde, an Irish Catholic already deep in
politics and also devoted to painting in several incongruous styles
at once, Byzantine and French. Affectation and enthusiasm were
so combined in him with insularity, and this with scraps of
exotic knowledge, that it was impossible for me to make out
whether he could be taken seriously in any direction. If you took
him seriously, he might have seemed a re-incarnation of Lionel
Johnson, this time genuinely Irish and at home in the political
world. If you took him for an intellectual ballet-dancer, he would
turn into the Lord Basil Kilcoole in my *The Last Puritan*; except
that Esmonde, when I knew him, was really young and handsome,
although his elegance was not borne out by everything in his
person, as it should be in a genuine beau. Beau Brummel would
have shuddered at the sight of those hands.

More my friend was the third of these youths, and he seemed
the youngest and least significant, Raymond Mortimer. He was
affectionate and literary, read my books, and took me out in a punt
to his favourite silvan resorts. He was an adoped child, perhaps a
foundling, and there was a certain mystery or ambiguity about his
whole person. He quoted to me the phrase "affected and disaffected" as describing him; but though disaffected politically, a
pacifist, and universal rebel, he was not affected: at least not
more than a young man must be who picks up a great deal that

he hadn't imbibed traditionally and without selecting it. Something of the waif, a prior grudge against everything, seemed to lurk in him, together with the assumption of universal competence: an attitude with which I have some sympathy, being myself something of a waif and a detached critic; but I see the inversion and folly in it, and its hollowness, because the order of nature is the contrary, and we must be true to ourselves before we can be just to other things, and consistently love our enemies. *The pure spirit* in us may safely cultivate universal sympathies; for it can have no grudge against anything and will be tender also to our accidental natural selves and our home world; but *the man* must remain loyal to himself and his traditions, or he will be morally a eunuch and a secret hater of all mankind.

I saw Mortimer later in Paris; and during a season I spent at the Hôtel du Palais Royal he would sometimes join me at ten in the evening at the Café de la Régence, where I usually had a *camomille* or a beer before turning in. France was perhaps more congenial to him than his own country: it was more of a universal vanity fair and intellectual market, where the surviving moral and national elements would be more hidden and less obstructive to a foreigner than they were in England. For this reason I too preferred to live in Paris and to read French books: not that, like Mortimer, I detested the old France or the old England, but because the new France afforded a more lucid medium through which to observe the dissolution of Christendom. This dissolution might be regretted; yet it was imperative to understand the forces and know the facts that were bringing it about. Harvard, also, if you were morally an outsider, afforded such a medium; but there, as in England, the intellectual grab-bag was offered by a missionary hand and with a single purpose, though perhaps an unconscious one: namely to equip everybody as well as possible in the service of national wealth and industrial dominance. The intellectual result, if you forgot that political purpose, was utter confusion; yet this chaos itself was welcome to the dilettante, the parasite, and the *viveur*. It enabled him to pick sweets out of the grab-bag at will, and to indulge all his impulses for the moment, yet sadly in the end: an intellectual brothel.

At Balliol those stray young men, with Urquhart and perhaps another Don or two, had formed an ephemeral club called the Thuliots which they asked me to join; and I had begun to scrawl a paper on ultimate things, to be read at the next meeting, when the wind that blew towards *Ultima Thule* seemed to die down. The term ended, and the next meeting never took place.

Like my first acquaintances at Oxford, so the last, were made through the Russells, pronounced anti-Oxonians. One day I received a telegram, signed *Russell,* asking me to come on a certain day to luncheon at a certain farm-house at Garsington. I replied accepting with pleasure, and unquestioningly addressed the telegram to Earl Russell; for I had no reason to expect such a message from Bertie. The next day a note came explaining that it was Bertie who had wired, and hoping I should come just the same. Of course I went, had to go; although it was a new excursion rather beyond my walking range, and involving a journey by the local line to a way station. I arrived duly; it was a real farm-house; and I found Bertie in a spacious upper chamber, with plank walls, and many books strewn about: but nothing about the landlady or the house seemed to forebode luncheon; and I had a good appetite. Presently Bertie said: "We'll go now to the Manor: I have my meals there." So we crossed the road and came to a renovated stone house, a bit below, which I hadn't noticed on arriving, and which proved to be a rather elaborate establishment, with a great garden. There, without previous explanation, I was introduced to a marvelous creature, very tall, very thin, in blue silk flounces, pearls, and black cross-garters (like Malvolio) over bright yellow stockings. She was Lady Ottoline Morrell, had an aristocratic nose, pale blue eyes, with dark straggling locks, and now appeared to be my hostess. She had a husband who I learned afterwards was a Liberal M.P. and a brother of my friend Mrs. Warren. Lady Ottoline had married the son of a brewer, and not an excessively rich one; but he was nice-looking, and her action, together with his politics, which came out at once in his talk, prepared me to understand how Bertie came to be there. Later I gathered that there was a very close old friendship, or perhaps a love-affair, between him and Lady Ottoline, which I know to subsist to this day. He was spending his holiday with the Morrells, but slept and worked at the farm-house for greater quietness and freedom.

I soon gathered that it was this lady, ostrich or tropical bird as she seemed, that had wished to discover me, and had caused Bertie to summon me. He and I have always been on pleasant terms, personally and intellectually; yet just as our philosophies are separate without being opposed, except in technicalities and in politics, so our lives and interests are separate, and we were never friends in the sense of looking each other up simply for pleasure or liking to live together. Lady Ottoline was an intellectual, and cultivated the society of intellectuals; it was in that capacity that she had heard of me, no doubt through Bertie or perhaps through Bridges, and thought of adding me to her collection.

If I had been younger and interested in forming acquaintances in England, I might have profited by her hospitality, and met various distinguished people at her house, such as Mr. Asquith, then Prime Minister. As it was, I came upon two notabilities worth mentioning: Lytton Strachey and Siegfried Sassoon. Strachey, who was then youngish, looked like a caricature of Christ; a limp cadaverous creature, moving feebly, with lank long brown hair and the beginnings of a beard much paler in colour, and spasmodic treble murmurs of a voice utterly weary and contemptuous. *Obscene* was the character written all over him; and his expertness in secret history and in satire expressed that character intellectually. That it was not merely intellectual appeared one day, when I found Lady Ottoline out, but expected, the maid said, to return shortly; and being left alone in the drawing room, I picked up a beautifully bound small book that lay at hand on the table. It was a French tale of the eighteenth century, and as obscene as possible. Naturally I read on in it, for I like obscenity well enough in its place, which is behind the scenes, or bursting out on occasion in a comic, rollicking, enormously hearty mood, as in Aristophanes; and when Lady Ottoline arrived, and found me reading it, she took pains to say it was not her book, but Mr. Strachey's. Certainly it wasn't likely to be her book; but he might have put it in his pocket, and not left it lying on the drawing-room table.

Siegfried Sassoon showed at first sight more of Siegfried than of Sassoon: a large blond young man sprawling in a large arm-chair, and saying little, as if he were dreaming of the mountains and the open fields. I saw him only once; but he obligingly drove me back to Oxford that afternoon, and from casual words he dropped and what I have seen of his poems, I daresay that the Sassoon side would soon have cropped out. He seemed to be swimming socially on the crest of every wave and to be universally informed, with moral chaos and bitterness beneath.

Lady Ottoline was most kind to me and I liked her the better the better I knew her; yet I resisted her invitations to stay at Garsington, and was repelled by the idea of nibbling the edges of her social and political world. It was the antithesis and the scornful enemy of the Oxford I could love. Unfortunately this lovable Oxford was imaginary or extinct or evanescent. It could be recaptured only in odd persons and stray glimpses. My bad scholarship, my Romanism, my connection with America and my friendship with the Russells made me unpalatable to the very people that I might have liked best. The conservatives and the poets had never heard of me, or wished they hadn't. Robert Bridges, Father Waggett, and Professor Stewart were the only exceptions; and I was not young enough to profit much by their friendliness. My path, thank God, had led me through Oxford, but it also, thank God, led me away from it.

# CHAPTER VI

## *FAREWELL TO ENGLAND*

IN the year 1919, when the peace of Versailles was being debated, Robert Bridges made a determined effort to induce me to settle for good in England. He said I had things to say that the English needed to hear. Save for the deference I always showed him, who was the only real friend I ever had much older than myself, I might have replied that it would be more becoming and more efficacious for *him* to say these things, if he thought them worth saying. He was poet laureate, official prophet to royalty, psalmist and vicar of King David. He knew the chords to strike and had the ear of the public; and if the public didn't pay much attention to him, what attention would they ever pay to me, a foreigner and a sceptic? Moreover, it was not my vocation to address the British public or any public, but to record as best I could the inwardness of things for a free spirit.

I loved England only too much. Living there I was in danger of losing my philosophical cruelty and independence. Omens of this contagion in sentiment, if not in doctrine, had already appeared in my little book on *Egotism in German Philosophy*; yet the English, far from being propitiated, only felt the more sharply the radical divergence of my mind from theirs. The reviewers accused me of debasing criticism into propaganda. That is what my position would have been in them, if they had assumed it: a philosophical inconsistency caused by political animus. They didn't understand, though they may have felt instinctively, that the egotism I attacked was far from being exclusively German, but was present in them and in the Americans whenever they turned their national ideal into something cosmic and eschatological, and felt themselves to be the chosen people. That if they did so they were themselves neither good philosophers nor good Christians was one of the things they needed to hear: but they wouldn't listen. Did Bridges himself understand it?

It was the net of Oxford that he spread in order to detain me. I had lived there off and on for five years, but absolutely unattached. The point now was to attach me, because I didn't conceal my intention of running away to Paris, to Spain, and to Italy. Now Bridges was a member of Corpus Christi College, and I had more than once been to luncheon there with him in the Senior Common Room; while F. R. S. Schiller, for many years, had asked me to dinner there in Hall, each time that I turned up at Oxford. Besides, a Boston acquaintance of mine, Edward Warren, was also living at Corpus; but he always invited me to his own rooms, where we might be tête-à-tête and freely discuss Boston and other delicate subjects. I was thus not unknown at Corpus; but now Bridges induced the Head of the College to ask me to luncheon, in order to inspect me. Apparently I passed muster. In those days I was thoroughly at home in the Oxford atmosphere of moderately comic anecdote—never roisterous—and sly hits at one another's heresies. A well-established Don, whose scholarship was impeccable, might like Conybeare cry across the table, if someone had asked what is orthodoxy, "Orthodoxy is reticence." But I knew better than to take such liberties. I smiled, and remembered the advice of Job to hold my peace, that peradventure I might be thought a wise man. At any rate a few days later Warren approached me with a confidential communication. He had been commissioned to sound me on the subject of residence in Oxford. Should I like to become, for life, a member of the High Table and Common Room at Corpus? For the moment, and during the war, they could let me have rooms in College, but in normal times all their rooms would be needed for undergraduates, and I should have to live in lodgings. When I politely shook my head, and gave merely civil reasons for declining, Warren asked—so little did he or the others understand me—whether I should prefer to teach. Oh, no: I had never wished to teach. I had nothing to *teach*. I wished only to learn, to be always the student, never the professor. And with being eternally a student went the idea of being free to move, to pass from one town and one country to another, at least while enough youth and energy remained for me to love exploration and to profit by it.

That was all true enough, but I had other far more decisive reasons for not accepting this invitation. Certainly it had a tempting side. I was happy in Oxford, and I needed a centre in which to keep my books and papers, and in which to hibernate and feel at home. The centre I had in Paris, and was about to return to, possessed certain advantages: it was cheap—as I was largely Strong's guest there—and it was convenient for Spain and Italy; yet rooms in an Oxford College, with the privileges of a Don, would have been far more comfortable and dignified. Had I had more money, I might have been seriously tempted to accept: but not at Corpus. Especially not ushered in there, as it were, by Warren, a Bostonian, and with Schiller every day at dinner, as my only other old friend. They were both individuals that a novelist might like to study, interesting cases; but to be sandwiched between them as if intellectually I were such another tramp (as externally indeed I was) would have been a perpetual mortification. Warren was unfortunate, yet I objected to him less than to Schiller, because I pitied him, and our connection with Boston was a true link; but Schiller, with the airs of a professed and shameless sophist, was an English Churchman, probably for that reason tolerated at Oxford where otherwise he might have been taboo. Perhaps it was his German blood that prevented him, in his simplicity, from seeing himself as others saw him. He earnestly presented himself as a candidate for *the professorship of logic in Oxford* and asked *me* to write a testimonial recommending him for that position!

Bridges, who understood me better, must have suspected that my refusal was based on reasons that I hadn't mentioned. Perhaps I didn't like Corpus, and should prefer another College. Now Bridges belonged also to New College, just the college to attract me: beautiful chapel, beautiful music, beautiful garden, old monastic cloisters, old city walls, classical traditions, High Church atmosphere, an undemolished statue of the Virgin still over the College Gate! It happens, that except Lionel Johnson and Bridges himself, I had never had a New College friend, while I have had so many at Balliol, Christ Church and Magdalene. But that would not have been an objection, if the present residents, masters and pupils, had proved sympathetic, as some of them surely would have done. Bridges on several occasions tried to introduce me to the Warden of New College, but I smelt a rat; perhaps I was afraid that I might be inveigled into some rash commitment. In any case I eluded all contacts in that direction, and so markedly, that I am afraid Bridges was a bit offended.

He said that my abandonment of England was "deplorable." Yet nothing was further from my thoughts than to "abandon" England. I hoped to return often, and I had never lived there except as a stranger and a guest. I was simply avoiding a misunderstanding, a false position. I could never abandon *my* England, because that was a part of myself, just as *my* America and *my* Spain are parts of myself: but these are not to be confused with the real, public, ever-changing England, Spain or America of geography and politics. My England was only the illusion with which the real England had inspired me. This illusion contained some truth; but it sprang from a few contacts, many of them indirect, and supplied by other poetic fictions. Shakespeare and Dickens were important sources, and especially Shakespeare's comedies and comic scenes in the histories and tragedies; for the histories officially depict mediaeval passions that are not English now, nor elements in my England. They are noisy. But in the songs, and in Shakespeare's wit and wistfulness everywhere, I find the spirit of my England purer than in any later poet. He was not puritan, he smacked of the country air and of young blood. I am well aware that the real England has many a virtue appreciable from points of view other than mine, virtues that are their own reward; but that is not my affair. It would have been treason to myself and a false profession of faith to have *wedded* the real England or the real America. They are variable material complexes; I could draw from them the pleasures and lessons of travel, but they are not ideal objects to which I would pledge my troth.

Mrs. Berenson once observed with feminine insight that my reasons for not living in England were not those which I gave out, such as my health, or the advantages of living with Strong in Paris or at Fiesole. My real reason, she said, was that England was too much like America. Not yet, perhaps, in 1920; but I felt in my bones, and divined everywhere, the tyrant flood of democracy in England and of commercial imperialism in America, visibly under-mining my England in England, and swallowing up my America in America. I was protecting, by fleeing from both, the memory of them in myself.

In these same months a suggestion that might have enticed me twenty-five years earlier came to me from a different quarter: it was that I should go to live as a paying guest with Howard Sturgis and the Babe. But twenty-five years earlier, Howard was rich and would not have dreamt of making me such a proposal, while I was poor, and could not have accepted it. Now the tables, in some measure, were turned. He was old, desolate, ill, and hard up; and I was a friend of long standing, free, with a comfortable income, and beginning to be esteemed as a writer. Moreover, I had always been on pleasant terms with the Babe, liked him, and didn't despise him for not being intellectual or for letting Howard adopt him and support him. If anything it was the Babe that was making the greater sacrifice; which indeed Howard would not have de-manded if his affection had been more heroic and his character less feminine. He could perfectly well have helped the Babe to find some comfortable post and to marry, and not have allowed him to grow old in an ambiguous dependence, and incidentally to waste Howard's fortune, not in riotous living but in foolish specu-lation. The Babe was certainly a minor personage, and feeble; but he kept his head and his spirits up in a difficult position, and was really the victim of the devotion that Howard insisted on show-ing him.

It was the Babe, on my last visit to them, who dropped a hint, evidently in consequence of confabulations that they had had together. Why didn't I settle down in England? Didn't I have a thousand pounds a year? No? Not so much? Anyhow, I could contribute a tidy sum, if I lived with friends who already had an establishment, but were suffering from the hard times. It would be so much more comfortable for me than living always in temporary quarters, in foreign countries, entirely alone.

How came Howard, with his knowledge of the world and of all his friends' weaknesses, to entertain such a project? He was living in the past. He saw himself, Queen's Acre, and me as we had been twenty-five years before. He knew how enchanting he and his circle had been to me then: a little Russian ballet in real life, great airs, extreme elegance in a diminutive setting, wide margins left on every side for glimpses of high life, of royalty, of politics, of poetry, of grotesque philosophy and grotesque morals; he himself a figurine, a voluntary caricature, sitting with his golden hair beautifully brushed, his small feet daintily crossed, in the middle of a square carpet on the emerald lawn, with his work-basket and menagerie of little dogs about him. His sparkling talk, while he embroidered some large design in gold thread, was alternately tender and merciless, mimicking and ridiculing everyone not present; yet he trembled, like a universal mother, at the mention of any illness, any death, any public disaster. And through all this a drift of charming relatives, guests, and casual visitors, all perfectly at home there, yet all in holiday mood, acting their various parts appropriately in the comedy and saying delicate things with a dancing mind.

The happy presence of reason in human life is perhaps better exemplified in comedy than in tragedy. In comedy we see no terrible sub-human or super-human fatality to render reason vain. Reason therefore can make its little runs and show its comic contradictions and clever solutions without disturbing the sound vegetative substance and free flowerings of human society. In comedy we laugh at our foolish errors, correct them with a word, and know no reason why we shouldn't be happy ever after.

Sparks of this free spirit of comedy flew constantly from Howard in his youth; but even then each spark threatened to be extinguished by a little suppressed gasp of compunction. Ridicule and pity seemed to chase each other in his mind. Where pity had the start, ridicule dropped out in despair; but when ridicule came first, as it usually did, pity was sure to overtake and smother it before the finish. Sentimental plays with comic relief do not make good comedy; and that was the trouble with Howard's life. He lacked genuine British stamina to keep him jolly in old age; and religion or genius would have been requisite to stiffen the sentimental side.

At Howard's the transformation had been gradual. Long before the war, during my summer visits, I had seen it approach. In 1890, when I first saw him at home, it seemed a bower of roses. He played by turns the fairy prince and the disconsolate Pierrot, now full of almost tearful affection, now sitting dressed in sky-blue silk at the head of his sparkling table, surrounded by young dandies and distinguished elderly dames; or when he drove his wagonette and high-stepping pair skilfully and festively, holding high the reins in his white-gloved hands, as if he were dancing a minuet.

Gradually all that joyfulness and gaiety had faded from the scene. First his fancy clothes were discarded: they had lost their freshness and perhaps they had got too tight, for he was no longer very slender. Anyhow masquerades at home were ridiculous and unsuitable. Then he gave up mimicking people, except involuntarily in little touches when he repeated what anyone had said. His imitations had been works of art, taking off not only voice and manner to perfection, but supplying diction and sentiments to suit, and only slightly exaggerated. But mockery, his aging conscience warned him, was unkind; and if he gave up being kind, what would remain of him?

The irony of fate would have it that now when he disciplined himself in kindness he was really far less kind than he had been when merry and ready to make fun of everybody; for just as he had loved lame little mongrel dogs for being lame and mongrel, so he had really loved us all in his youth for being absurd and full of little weaknesses; whereas now the merry sentimentalist had become a melancholy one, and sadly censorious. And while the freedom and light faded from his spirit, the sunshine seemed also to fade from his garden and the joyousness from his house. Anticipations had not been realised. The house had been enlarged, but seemed smaller, the furniture old-fashioned and worn, the once flowering garden grey and bald like our respective heads. The ribaldry had been expunged from conversation, but also the wit, the frankness, the variety. Any straggling guest like myself caused evident disturbance. I knew that some white wine had been ordered expressly on my arrival, so that it might not seem that there was nothing to drink. If I came to live with them I should be an expense, as well as a help: nor could it be an act of kindness on my part in other ways, because our views now clashed not in merriment any longer but in displeasure. People do not grow better when they grow older; they remain the same, but later circumstances cause them to exhibit their character sometimes in a minor key with the soft pedal, so that they seem to us grown sweeter, and sometimes more harshly and disagreeably, when we think them soured or depraved. No: we are no longer charmed by their virtues or interested in their vices.

With the lapse of years Howard and I had begun to see each other in this less favourable light. He thought I was abominably selfish. Certainly, I am profoundly selfish in the sense that I resist human contagion, except provisionally, on the surface, and in matters indifferent to me. For pleasure, and convivially, I like to share the life about me, and have often done it; but never so as, at heart, to surrender my independence. On the other hand, I am not selfish in a competitive way. I don't want to snatch money or position or pleasures from other people, nor do I attempt to dominate them, as an unselfish man would say, for their own good.

I sincerely wish them joy in their native ways of living, as if they were wild animals; but I decidedly refuse to hunt with them unless the probable result recommends itself to me independently.

To heartlessness of this kind I am ready to plead guilty, and see clearly that it is inhuman. Sympathy with nature, however, is the source of it, and not any aggressive selfishness. Every need or passion evokes dramatic sympathy; but the contrariety among the passions gives that sympathy pause and evokes reason. Now reason, confronted with the chaos and hell of all these conflicting passions and needs, often takes a Mephistophelian turn. Reason can never be malignant, because it is a complex of sympathies, but it may sometimes be cynical, when it shows how many needs are needless and how many passions artificial. I confess that I often like the sayings of Mephistopheles and Iago as much as I dislike the conduct of Othello and Faust. In those sayings there is light; but in the action of those heroes there is no light, only the blind will of protoplasm to stir and to move on, or the blind error of a bull fighting a shadow. As to the action of Mephistopheles or Iago, there is properly none. There is no human motive for it, only the traditions of a puppet show, with devils popping up to do the mischief. And this explains the inhumanity of these stage villains. They develop reasoning in the modern drama without possessing the generic animal needs and passions requisite to evoke reason in any creature. Reason can serve to control and harmonise such natural interests; it cannot take their place.

I happened to be at Queen's Acre in 1914 shortly after the outbreak of war, when Howard was suffering from a cruel sense of the folly of mankind. What could be more senseless than destruction, destruction, destruction? Yet in his intense liberalism he had applauded the destruction of ancient institutions and ways of life, because destruction there had made room for liberty. The destruction of modern works, on the contrary, would make for poverty; and like a true child of the Great Merchants, Howard was convinced that riches exalted worthy people and made them beneficent. Destruction is indeed cruel and odious when it is carried on for its own sake, malignantly or covetously, like the destruction of the monasteries during the Reformation and the revolutions still to-day malignant; but if we take a broad cosmic view of destruction it is only the shady side of progress. Like natural death it is inevitable; and though we regret it when premature or needlessly painful, there would be as much sentimental folly in disallowing it as in mourning the coming on of night or of autumn.

So the war of 1914–18 was intended by the Germans to be, for them and for the future of the world, a step in individual and political progress; and so too the next war, wickedly destructive and arrogant on both sides, was conceived, first again by the Germans, and then by all the combatants. The Great Merchants' wealth and the whole economic system of which they were the flower, proved in fact less beneficent and much less durable than the *ancien régime*. Howard himself was a pathetic victim of this system; he was generosity and refinement personified; but he couldn't help envying the dying aristocracy that he imitated and denounced; and the necessary soil to sustain his wealth, refinement, and generosity slipped visibly from under his feet.

During that first climacteric war, I heard that Howard had taken lodgings in London in order to do "War Work" by reading, censoring and readdressing German prisoners' correspondence. This was a marked sacrifice of his comfort and leisure; but solitary comfort with moral irritation and loneliness is not happiness; and the change of scene, the dutiful occupation, and the sense of helping to console mothers, sweethearts, and wives was surely some compensation, in spite of possible bombs. But there was a tragic background to this charitable act. Howard was beginning to suffer from a mortal illness, cancer in the bowels; and although he had been reprieved by one dangerous operation, another was destined to be necessary. Fortune proved faithless to him with a vengeance; but he showed a remarkable fortitude, not stoical but tender. The fountains of pleasure and gaiety, so sparkling in his youth, had run dry. It was not difficult to surrender the world, when the affections remained which alone need never be surrendered.

When months later, in Italy, I saw in *The Times* that Howard was dead, and on writing to the Babe received assurances that Howard had died peacefully, without pain, and nobly resigned, then the whole long and curious chapter of my friendship with him came up before me, much as I have recorded it here; and I was glad that the end, which had to be sad, at least had not been harrowing. If I had jumped at the chance of going to live at Queen's Acre, thinking I had found a home at last, my illusion would have been short-lived, and our brief life in common would not have been happy. Still, when I returned to England in 1923, I went to see the Babe where he was living with his father near Bath; but it was an unsatisfactory postscript. What ghastly pleasure this is, to pull the dead out of their graves! My morning tea was served me in a beautiful china cup, one of a familiar set in the old days at Howard's, now apparently the last survivor, glued and rivetted together in many places, like a mutilated veteran of the Guard. Was I sorry that Howard was dead? No: but I was glad that he had lived. And here I repeated the experience of my uncle Santiago on the death of his daughter. "I had already lost her," he said, "when she was married." I had already, gradually and insensibly lost Howard when he began to shed his rare self, with its inimitable honest mixture of effeminacy and courage, sensibility and wit, mockery and devoted love.

Meantime, a curiously similar cloud had obscured my other chief friendship, my other Mecca, in England. Russell too had become estranged and resentful; and here also, while there was no open breach, there could be no pleasure or simplicity in keeping up the old intimacy. I have described already the circumstances and the issue of this misunderstanding: if now I compare what happened there with what had happened to me with Howard Sturgis, I see a fundamental difference. With Howard the chief trouble was that we had both grown old, that the natural period of our intimacy was past, and could not be prolonged honestly. Howard complained of this, because he was motherly, tender, affectionate, and jealous. He would have wished the Babe to be always a babe, and me to be always the delighted young traveller. I made no such claims, and felt only the melancholy that pervades a world where everything is transitory. By that time I was inured to the cyclical character of all my friendships, that set a period to the best of them, sometimes a very brief one. For me this involved no estrangement, no disillusion; on the contrary, the limits of each friendship perfected that friendship, insured it against disaster, enshrined it in the eternal. Spirit can immortalise events without being able to prolong them; it can virtually survey all seasons at every season. That is what I am doing now to my love of England and of my English friends. My farewell to them, in so far as it was my doing, was only temporal; they belonged to my past; materially we had to separate; it was better and wiser to do so in time. In that way nothing need grow stale, nothing need lapse or contradict itself or confuse the affections.

With Russell the bond had little to do with externals, whether in our persons or in our circumstances. Conventionally, without the quickness and simplicity of youth, we should never have become friends; and many people always wondered how it could have happened. The affinity between us lay beneath the surface, and I, at least, felt it at once very strongly: and in two directions. There was physical or vital affinity, or rather attraction by contrast: I admired his fearlessness, agility, and skill in doing things entirely beyond my powers; and he found me sympathetic and calm. Then, intellectually, in independent and disinterested judgment, we coincided: but since this was only a transcendental identity, it could pass unobserved, and could seem to be destroyed by our contrary prejudices in concrete matters. Nevertheless this double affinity could hardly be affected by the lapse of time: and I think that if Russell had finished his career in the world as early as I did, before the age of fifty, we might have been ideal old cronies in our declining years, grumbling of course at each other, yet perfectly happy together. But before he was rid of his matrimonial embarrassments, he had plunged into the troubled waters of unsuccessful business and unsuccessful politics; and he succumbed, exhausted, in the heat of the day, without ever feeling the cool of the twilight. I on the contrary have been enjoying peace for thirty years, in the midst of prodigious wars. In regard to Russell, I had really been guilty of an indiscretion in questioning the wisdom of his change of wives, when his mind was probably made up. But my motive had been sympathy with his new love, not disapproval; and I feared that legal commitments towards both wives at once would lead to a catastrophe. Had he and Elizabeth retained their freedom, the episode might have ended in comparative peace. Undoubtedly, on the day when Elizabeth had come for me at the station, to win me for her cause, Russell could reasonably have said "Allow that you were a fool. You didn't know Elizabeth, and you couldn't conceive how happy she would be with me." But soon *she was not happy*; and her unhappiness led her to confide in me, and deepen the sympathy naturally inspired by her delicate mind and person. Russell perceived this, and disliked it; his displeasure even became a kind of jealousy. Not that he imagined for a moment that Elizabeth and I were making love; that would have been absurd; but we seemed to be more confidential and sympathetic about him than with him. This was unfortunately the case, entirely against our will and expectation. We were both interested only in him, and troubled about what threatened to cloud our relations with him or, in her case, to make them impossible. I couldn't help recognising her difficulties, and the qualities in him that could cause them: to me they were an old story and I had, as he knew, foreseen them and warned him of what would happen. That this should now irritate him, was only human; but here a confusion seems to have arisen in his mind. He thought that I too had become *hostile* to him; that I was *abandoning* him and becoming her ally. He was angry because I saw her once or twice in London after she had left him. He seemed to demand that I should break with her, and because I refused to do so, he said I was "disloyal."

There was a marked peculiarity in Russell's mind that helps to explain this misunderstanding. Perspectives for him were strictly limited: he saw only what, for the moment, touched the matter in hand. All the rest of the truth lapsed altogether. He used to say in the early years that he cared nothing for what his friends might do when he wasn't present. I noticed, for instance, even when he seemed glad to have me as a companion, that he never remembered that any such things existed as my family, my prospects, my opinions, or my books. I was nothing but what I was *for him*. Far from resenting this, I had liked it. It helped me also to shed my past and my future, and to live for the moment in another's life. I was being treated justly and generously in my capacity of friend available for that occasion; I was not meddled with, judged, or misrepresented in my other capacities.

It is characteristic of spontaneous friendship to take on trust, without enquiry and almost at first sight, the unseen doings and unspoken sentiments of our friends: the part known gives us evidence enough that the unknown parts cannot be much amiss. Nor does this imply that the unknown parts must be intelligible to us or after our own taste; on the contrary, it is almost better that they should extend into the inimitable. Friendship may then be touched at the edges with admiration and love. Russell knew that I was a being apart, dependent on him for nothing except the pleasure of his society; he was well aware that in politics my views were different from his: not contradictory but at another level. I never aired them; and I heartily enjoyed the satirical expositions he would make of English law, custom, and prejudice. I learned a lot from him, and was silently confirmed in my silent affections and philosophy. We never argued. If by chance our divergences came to the surface, he grunted and I laughed. I knew that English opinions had to grow like that, with the scent and the promise of fruit; they were instrumental or edifying opinions, and it would have been unprofitable for them to bother to be true. I on my side was allowed to remain ineffectual and negligible in my wise fool's paradise.

Russell's indifference to everything not involved in his present surroundings or sentiments produced odd lapses in his memory. I

have mentioned his forgetting altogether that I had pulled him
into the water at Richmond, something that at the time had in-
furiated him. This might conceivably have been suppressed by
Freud's "Censor"; there were other cases of forgetfulness regarding
inconvenient or regrettable facts that, in early days, he himself
had told me of; and here the pressure of a later *parti pris* evidently
had first ignored and then erased the contrary memory. Yet in
general it was more what Bergson describes: urgent practical business absorbing attention and driving irrelevant ideas from con-
sciousness. Russell's worries fatigued, distracted and harrowed his
mind. A curious sign of this, in his last years, was that he repeatedly called me Sargeaunt. Sargeaunt was a Latin master at
Westminster, the translator of Terence in *Loeb's Classics*, who no
doubt had been a friend of Russell's at school or in Oxford, and
who sometimes came for a week-end to T.H. They had nothing
now in common save that old sense of familiarity. This was incidentally what, from his present point of view, Russell saw in me.
Both Sargeaunt and I were obviously inoffensive, unimportant
elderly persons shuffling about abstractedly: both teachers and old
bachelors and old acquaintances, who knew his ways and were not
nuisances, and whose names began with an S and had A's and
N T's in them. Sargeaunt or Santayana, what difference did it
make?

No doubt this was only a slip of the tongue, in moments of
abstraction. A Freudian treatment would have elicited that I had
been the only one of his old friends, besides his brother, to stick
to him openly through thick and thin for thirty years; that I had
been the witness or confidant of many of his love-affairs (though
not all of them) and had given testimony for him in the most
scandalous of his law-suits, without a thought of the possible risk
to my own reputation and livelihood. But all this lay in the past,
hidden by the fog of the present, and to be brought to light only
at the Last Judgment. To see now only what counted now was
a sign of being a man of action and a good politician. And in his
life now I counted for very little; perhaps at last I had even become
a nuisance.

Yet at the very time when he was confusing me with Sargeaunt, he was complaining that I was "disloyal" and this reproach pre-supposes allegiance. It asserts regal claims that only long years of fidelity could justify: so that the past remained virtually present *in him,* though banished from his conscious memory. Precisely because he knew that I was loyal, he was hurt to find that I under-stood Elizabeth's grievances and rebellion. *I* had no grievances, *I* was not deserting him; and in his last letter to me, dictated a week before his death, he crossed out the secretary's word "sin-cerely" at the end and wrote as usual, "Yours ever."

When I returned to England in 1923 I had written to him announcing my presence and asked if he wished me to go and see him. He replied "Do as you like." I went for a short week-end. He was alone, and spent his day, as he had always done, exactly as if I hadn't been there. I found him busy over the wires of his new radio—it was then a novelty—and in the evening, without dressing, we went to dine at a retired Admiral's in a neighbouring village, where Russell, with his radio, was to give a talk to the villagers at the church vestry or school-house. The radio didn't work very well; it refused to connect with Paris, as Russell had planned; but a fragment of a fragment of a music hall performance in London was heard with satisfaction and wonder. On Sunday we went for a long motor drive; I was not forewarned, but I found that we were bound to a particular cottage where an interesting widow was expecting us for tea. She and Russell afterwards strolled aside in earnest and somewhat troubled conversation. Evidently the course of true love here didn't run smooth. Five years had passed since the flight of Elizabeth and I ought to have expected to find a lady in the picture. No doubt he had a secretary or other com-panion in London; but that wasn't enough. He was haunted by the need of a happy home.

The next morning he took me back to town in his motor: and here there was a significant change. It was a closed motor, that is to say, it had a glass front and a roof, but Russell drove and I sat beside him as usual on the front seat. However, there was a chauffeur, something not known formerly; and Russell said that now he sometimes let him drive while he himself dozed on the back seat. He was tired. For thirty years he had lived a distracted life under high pressure and a forced draught, a life absorbed not in doing what he was fit to do but in getting rid of obstacles and wasting his energies on trifles and his affections on impossible women. He needed relaxation, yet couldn't relax. He never drank: a glass of wine would upset him. Continual discomfort had crept into his system; it would be soothed or forgotten only by the greater strain of fast motoring or playing cards, with stakes rather higher than he could afford. For he had become poor; law-suits and losses in business had nearly ruined him; he was kept going precariously by being director of various precarious companies. He had forgotten his youthful cultivated tastes; he had lost his old friends; he had repudiated his wives or been abandoned by them.

Luckily politics, his hereditary calling, came after a fashion to the rescue. He was elected to the London County Council, and afterwards played a useful if not distinguished part in the House of Lords and in the Government. But for me this was small comfort. I knew what a sham it all was, how unhappy it left him, how it buried the truly masterful side of him under a load of ridiculous servitudes. He thought life had to be like that; that it was a rough, fast game you must play; after which your ashes should be scattered to the winds. Peace would come soon enough in death. He could not conceive peace to be something positive, like laughter or intelligence, that lived in the midst of life and was the true triumph over it. Yet he had possessed that peace in his first youth most emphatically; and we had enjoyed it together.

Such, on the sentimental side, and in regard to my friends, was my farewell to England. I recognised that that chapter was closed. I yet expected to return often to England, and to revisit my old haunts there, and find other pleasant places. I might see them in an autumnal colouring; that would be a new beauty; it might almost be worth the old. I should stop in London only in transit, but revisit Oxford, Cambridge, Windsor, and perhaps even T.H. for the old solitary walks over fields and downs, or by quiet rivers.

All this was not to be, and I am glad of it. Materially, however, I did return to England twice, and for a tell-tale reason. I was invited to give lectures. The author, the professor went; the spirit did not accompany him. The first time was in 1923 when they asked me to give the Herbert Spencer lecture at Oxford. I was glad to accept; this was my first and last official connection with that University. The question might be what to say about Spencer, whom I had not read or thought of since my undergraduate days, when William James lectured about him. To have reread Spencer would have been too severe a penance; I chose *The Unknowable* for a subject, as admitting no investigation. I chose also the earliest possible date in October for my lecture, so as to get back to Italy before the winter set in. However, with my romantic notion of revisiting old haunts, and composing elegies about *La Chute des Feuilles*, I went, as I have already related, to see Russell; and Howard being dead I went to see the Babe, and then retired to lodgings in Cambridge in order to finish writing my lecture. There the always amiable Lapsley put me up at the High Table at Trinity, where I had pleasant conversations with Mac-Taggart and with Housman. But I was not well, persecuted by my bronchial catarrh, and without heart to re-evoke any Oxford ghosts.

There, I went to the Clarendon Hotel, walked one day to Iffley, and saw nobody except young Randolph Chetwynd, who was charming, but busy trying to argue I don't know what socialists back to liberalism. He lived in an old stable or coach-house in New College Lane which had been turned into chambers: the sloping roof was open to the eye, plastered, and made picturesque by beams painted black and by iron brackets and lanterns. He dined with me at my hotel and after dinner left me alone to sit by his fire, with a glass of port, and a book said to be interesting; but no, I couldn't feel at home. Nor was my age the only cause. Oxford also was not itself. I couldn't walk through New College Lane or Merton Lane without being startled, as by a cavalry charge, by troops of young women on bicycles, wearing caps and gowns. Was it worth while for Randolph to stem the tide of Socialism? Better let the flood come, I thought, and perhaps something genuine after its kind might emerge after the deluge.

As to my lecture, it was kindly received, but by the oddest of audiences in the oddest of places. I never felt less in Oxford at Oxford than on that occasion. I had been put in communication with a scientific Don, doubtless of the Committee for the Spencer Lectureship; and when I called at his house by appointment an hour before the time for the lecture, his wife said he was so sorry but he had been called away to receive 4000 butterflies that had just arrived from South America. He turned up later, however, and took me to the Natural History Museum, not to see the butterflies, but to read my lecture in a hall like an operating-theatre, with a deep pit, and great blackboards and maps on the walls. He wore no gown and instead of introducing me said simply, "Oh you might as well begin." The audience, sprinkled about the steep semi-circle of seats, comprised a good many Indians and Japanese, and a few ladies. I recognised only old Professor Stewart, always most kind to me, and F. R. S. Schiller. This audience, however, soon became sympathetic, perceived that they were expected to laugh, and applauded heartily at the end. Several dusky youths brought me books to be autographed. Did they feel that I was one of them at heart? We might have been in Singapore.

This occasion had been graceless externally, but morally it left a pleasant impression. I felt that my labour had not been wasted. Not so the evening before, when I had been invited to dine at Wadham and to read a paper before a philosophical club. I had nothing with me except the first chapter of *The Realm of Essence,* so I read that. There was no sympathy in the air, and I read without warmth. When it came to the discussion everybody seemed at sea, and caught at phrases or trifles that struck them as odd. Nobody had heard of *Scepticism and Animal Faith,* published not long before. Samuel of New College, Robert Bridges' son-in-law, but white-bearded like a Hebrew prophet, observed sarcastically that "there seemed to be a thing called substance."

Only one little chap, perhaps an Irishman or a Catholic, said something that showed comprehension. How glad I was not to be at New College with the Prophet Samuel and the Prophet Joachim! Wasn't I at heart more English than these "Englishmen" and more Oxonian than these Oxonians? How much at home I should have felt in fleeing from them to Harold Fletcher and Father Waggett, to old Higgs and Robert Bridges!

A thousand silent isolated wits, if I could have got at them, would not only have understood my philosophy but would have fortified my love of England and of mankind. But my lot was cast among the heretics and the radicals, and I seemed insignificant to the professional idealogues who had never had the courage to face the cruel truth about anything, much less to utter it.

There was then a through train direct from Oxford to Dover, passing through the pleasant hilly country south of the Thames and avoiding London. I took it the next morning and found it most comfortable and almost empty. Apparently it was not yet the season for continental travel from Liverpool and the North; but it was lovely autumnal weather, pleasant to the eyes and suitable for a timely but still affectionate farewell to England.

Nevertheless I returned nine years later for another visit. I had agreed to go in September, to the Spinoza Tercentennial meeting at the Hague, and had already finished my address for that occasion when I received an invitation from the Royal Society of Literature in Bloomsbury Square to speak to them about Locke, born, like Spinoza, in 1632. Holland is not far from England geographically or morally, and after my heavy work on Spinoza it would be entertaining to write something lighter about the English worthy. The meetings at the Domus Spinozana had pleased me: I had paid my homage to the *numen* of the place, I had learned something about my hero, namely, how *theological* his youth had been (just like mine) and I had breathed gladly again the air of the Netherlands, their vast horizons and their homely ways. I would risk crossing the North Sea, and would ask Cory, who was in London, to engage rooms for me somewhere at St.

James's, where I should feel at home. I didn't mean to leave town or to revive any sentimental associations. Oxford was vulgarised, Cambridge was stale, Russell was "dead and cremated." I would devote the mornings to finishing my lecture, and get some book—it happened to be Aldous Huxley's latest—to while away the evenings; Cory would come to lunch with me every day at Hatchett's, and then I would go for a solitary walk in Hyde Park, and a comfortable tea before turning in. I carried out this programme to the letter. My rooms in St. James's Place were not like lodgings in Jermyn Street of old: bad service, gas fires (at which I had to finish toasting my toast in the morning, holding it with a fork) and a dismal outlook over mews and chimney-pots. Besides I was suffering from my bronchial catarrh, not severely, but enough to mar the pleasure of mere existence. However, I should have ended my visit in a neutral state of somnambulism, but for the disgusting experience of the day of my lecture.

This lecture was a *jeu d'esprit*, it was gay, it was addressed to the free and unprejudiced mind. It also presupposed a certain familiarity with the quality of modern ideologies, seen satirically. I had counted on an audience like the blessed one at the British Academy in 1918 who laughed merrily when they heard that, for a pragmatist, the real past was the idea of the past that he would have in the future. But I found a Bloomsbury audience that didn't consent to smile. Nor was it intellectual opacity alone that enveloped me. All the lights in the room were in my eyes and none on the reading desk. I had purposely brought my own manuscript, written large and clear on alternate lines, but I couldn't see to read it. What was I to do? Finally, by having the lights at the rear of the room put out, I found that I could manage, though with great difficulty and uncertainty. Sir Rennell Rodd (not yet a peer), who had been Ambassador at Rome, pompous and vacuous, introduced me in a vague little speech, saying nothing about Locke and repeatedly calling me a-a-a thinker and a-a-a writer, fortunately not a-a-a professor. It was evident that he knew nothing about me. Disgusted as I was about the lights, and chilled by the chairman and the audience, I couldn't fall into the spirit of my paper, or assume the facile and confidential tone that it demanded. However, I pulled through somehow, and at the end I was surprised that they applauded with some persistence, as if to say: "Your lecture was a bit queer and disconcerting in places, and we haven't quite caught the drift of it; but we realise that it was a superior lecture, as lectures go." Even Sir Rennell Rodd, in his speech of thanks, had a happy thought. He observed, between two little pauses, that perhaps there was subtlety in what I had said. Yes, Sir Rennell; there were insinuations.

When we broke up, an Indian came to ask me some leading questions about Locke. He wished to be confirmed in thinking Locke superficial. When I explained that Locke was a pioneer, more important in his influence than in his insight, my dusky friend showed his white teeth. Yes, he said, Locke wasn't *profound*. A lady also came up who said that she was Mrs. Inge and that her husband had been sorry not to be able to come and hear me. When I spoke of my sympathy with the Dean's views on the history of religion, and my debt to his *Plotinus*, she shifted the subject at once, repeating how much he liked what I had written about *the English character*. Was it entirely as poetry, as description, as analysis that those words of mine in the *Soliloquies* were so often noticed? Are they juster than what I said of other things? I am afraid they were valued a little as testimonials. The English now had begun to relish praise even from an obscure foreigner! I am confirmed in this suspicion by the fact that Bertrand Russell, who retained the old British pride in Baconian England, its science, philosophy, and politics, actually resented my sentimentality about the *boyish* Englishman, and complained that I cared for nothing except undergraduates and the families they came from. Quite so: there I found human virtue pure and not distorted by any fanaticism, intellectual or moral, or by any shams.

After this unpleasant last visit, my farewell to England seemed almost an escape. It was a relief to feel that this chapter, rich as it had been, was closed forever. It was like burying a wife

long ago divorced: there was peace in the finality of it. No more
attempts to patch things up, no more fresh disappointments to
cloud the memory of old embraces. For I had once embraced
England with a deep and quiet pleasure. She had seemed perfect
in her simplicity, in her distinction, in the comfort of her ways.
How decent, how wise, how gentle these ways had been, how
beautiful her eyes and voice, how healthful her affections! And
although I was avowedly a wayfarer, not fit to be her acknowl-
edged lover or husband, yet she had sometimes seemed to love
me a little. She had understood that I was to be trusted, that I saw
things as they were, and was not shocked at the truth. She had
felt that I loved her as a poet should love, without claims, without
flattery, and with an incurable pang in his unfeigned rapture.

# CHAPTER VII

## OLD AGE IN ITALY

WHEN at the threshold of old age I found myself free and looked about for a place of retirement and finally found it in Italy and particularly in Rome, I was not at all in search of an ideal society or even of a congenial one. I was looking only for suitable lodgings, where the climate, the scene, and the human ways of my neighbours might not impede but if possible inspire me in my projected work and where I might bring my life to a peaceful end. As to society, I was quite content with that which naturally surrounded me; for I still had my family and my friends in America, in England, and in Spain; while in Italy later the Anglo-American residents, with their fringe of distinguished Italian acquaintances, would have been accessible to me if I had cared to cultivate them more assiduously. But essentially I desired solitude and independence: not in the English form of quiet home life in the country, but rather after the fashion of ancient philosophers, often in exile, but always in sight of the market-place and the theatre.

Nor was I at first entirely adrift. Even my relations with Harvard were not suddenly severed. President Lowell had resisted my wish to resign and we had come to an agreement that, after eighteen months' leave, I should return for the first half of each year. I meant to carry out this plan so long as my mother lived; but she died soon after my departure, and my sister Josefina returned to live in Spain. I had henceforth no home in America. At the same time my income was somewhat increased, and I resigned my professorship by letter. The question of an official residence thus presented itself immediately, and remained more or less open during the next ten years.

My nominal headquarters, as well as my books, remained for some time at Strong's in the Avenue de l'Observatoire, and my passport was periodically renewed by the Spanish Consulate in Paris. But Strong and I were never there in winter, and he usually went in summer to see his parents. Sometimes I spent a season there alone, in a silence most favourable for concentration of mind. Then, in the evening, I could remember that all Paris lay at my feet, behind that screen of green trees, and I would go to the Boulevards or to the Champs Elysées for a stroll and for dinner.

There was evidently no finality, no sense of home, in such a *pied à terre*. Nor was Paris a place where, even if I had been younger and richer, I should have cared to live. It did very well for an occasional season of cosmopolitan pleasures, but even its intellectual and artistic movements, though they greatly attracted and rewarded attention, were episodes, fashions, and extravagances with which no one would wish to be identified. Even distinguished and philosophical persons that I came across never inspired any confidence in my mind. Three of these might be mentioned: Bergson, Boutroux, and Dr. Cazalis, who wrote under the name of Jean Lahore. None of these were Catholics, so that in them all there was a certain strain of self-consciousness, as of outsiders who always felt a little aggrieved and a little insincere in the French atmosphere. I have never had a French friend. In the most charming of them I felt something false, as if an evil spell bound them to some secret and sinister cause, and they were feigning all their amiability for an ulterior reason. They could never be disinterested, never detached. They had in their hearts a sort of covert intensity and stubborn nearsightedness that I could not endure. On the other hand I have fed with perpetual delight on the French way of putting things: everything was perceived by them, everything tolerated, nothing overdone, nothing insisted upon. The French mind is an exquisite medium for conveying such things as can be communicated in words. It is the unspoken things of which one feels the absence or mistrusts the quality.

During my first three years I instinctively turned to Spain, and besides long visits in Avila, I lived awhile with Mercedes in Madrid, in a circle composed of twenty-seven women and not one man. For partial relief, I then went with her and Josefina to Seville. After a while they were bored there, and left me to enjoy the air in the gardens, the Cathedral, the little plays at 10.30 at the *Teatro del Duque,* the bull-fights, and the processions of Holy Week. I even went sometimes to the music hall *Novedades* to see the local dancing and hear the local songs. It was well enough for once, or for the young natives who can enjoy it all gracefully, and escape to higher things. But for me, with my tastes and at my age, it was only a flimsy spectacle, a surface without volume or depth and with nothing to hold me. During another winter, being cold and bored in Madrid with Mercedes and her intimates, I made a trip to Valencia, Alicante, and Murcia. I saw some lovely spots along the coast, where a Spanish *Riviera* might exist; but the towns and the life were distinctly second-rate, and even the language, as far as Murcia, not Castilian. Avila, I perceived, was the only place in Spain where I might live happily. I kept that in reserve; for the moment I would look about elsewhere. Before long, however, war had broken out, and by chance had caught me in Cambridge at the *Red Lion*; and in England I remained for five years.

When I returned to Avila after the war I felt a distinct change in the moral climate. My long residence in England and the fact that my sympathies during the struggle had been strong on the English side, produced a chill towards me in my sister's family. Their sentiments had been, and continued always to be, inspired by clerical and nationalist Spanish opinion, which anticipated what it became during the second general war. At that time I didn't altogether appreciate the grounds of such violent Anglophobia. It was not founded on knowledge of England, as my feelings were. It arose indirectly, through traditional fear and hatred of English influence in other European countries; and to this was added the detestation of French influence in Spain both in politics and in religion. These good people did not suspect (although the Pope did) that modern Germany was more anti-Catholic than England or even than republican France, in that it preached an enthusiastic return to heathenism; whereas England and France were merely Erastian, worldly, greedy and money-loving, as the Catholic soul of Castile certainly was not. The Latin peoples did not preach a racial war based like the Teutonic claims on the Jewish foundations of Christianity, nor propose to saddle a Nietzschean morality on peaceful lands like Austria, Bavaria, and the Rhineland that were traditionally Catholic.

Not that my own philosophy was partisan or afraid of Nietzsche. Neither tribal nor commercial morality inspired me with particular horror. I knew that the first was brutal and the second vulgar; but they both were intelligible phases in human civilisation, just as Catholicism was; and it was an accident of temperament or circumstances how far my sympathies were enlisted on one or the other side. Essentially I could sympathise with them all, but could identify myself with none. That I was a philosopher, that I could identify myself willingly only with intelligence and with the truth, offended my friends in Avila, as it now seems to offend some of my friends in other places.

The idea of eventually living in Avila, with one of my sisters or with both, remained with me; but the moment had not arrived. Meantime I would make trial of the Riviera, the common refuge of the lazy in exile; and I took rooms with only first breakfast served, first at Monte Carlo and then in Nice, going to Italian restaurants for my other meals. I should have liked the old town of Monaco, with its gardens overhanging the sea, but there was no hotel there, and no likely lodgings. In Nice I had a bad attack of my chronic catarrh, and moved to a clinic, where lying comfortably in bed by a wide open window, I had a pleasant convalescence spent reading Spengler's *Untergang des Abendlandes,* all but the mathematical part, which I couldn't understand and distrusted *a priori*; for it is a marvel that mathematics should apply so well to the material world, and to apply it to history or ideas is pure madness.

The atmosphere of the Riviera, physical and moral, didn't agree with me very well. And the same may be said of Florence, in spite of the presence there of some old friends, Strong, Loeser, and Berenson. They, Strong especially, with his new villa, caused me often to stop there, as I never did again at the Riviera; yet even in Fiesole I was never happy. All nationalities are better at home, where they are less conspicuous as special nationalities, and may pass for common humanity. When you transplant the species, it suffers constraint and becomes sickly or intrusive or both at once. I like to be a stranger myself, it was my destiny; but I wish to be the only stranger. For this reason I have been happiest among people of all nationalities who were not of my own age, class, or family circle; for then I was a single exceptional personage in their world, and they a complete harmonious milieu for me to drop into and live with for a season. Where there were other foreigners among whom I was classed, and with whom I was expected to be more at home than with the natives, I was ill at ease in both camps, and disliked each for not knowing how to live with the other. For this reason in America I avoided all foreigners, especially all Spanish people; and in England or Spain or even Italy, I suffered when I was with Americans. Only in Paris, a cosmopolitan caravansary in itself, did Americans and other foreigners fall nicely into the picture and spoil nothing in the charm of the place. This would probably not have been the case even there, if I had known the best French people: but I saw only persons already cultivating foreigners and making up to them for interested reasons; and it was not among such that I cared to move.

It might seem that I turned to Italy and especially to Rome as a last resort, but that was not the case. Italy and Rome were my first choice, my ideal point of vantage in thought, the one anthropological centre, where nature and art were most beautiful, and mankind least distorted from their complete character. But I had wished to look about first to see if my own country, or places more allied to my later associations, like England, would not be, for me, more desirable retreats: for it was a retreat I was looking for, not a field of action. No: upon trial I was sure that none of them would be better. Therefore I began to spend my winters in Rome in 1920, as I have done ever since. For the summer I still went to Paris, to Avila, sometimes to Glion over the lake of Geneva, a short walk to the clinic where Strong often took refuge. But I remembered the terms in which my poetic friend Stickney had eulogised Cortina, an ideal Tyrolese village in an emerald-green valley amid the mountains of the moon; and now, after the war, Cortina was in Italy. I tried it, going to the Hotel Cristallo high on a hillside. It was here, in a bare little bedroom on the top floor, that I wrote at one stretch, *Platonism and the Spiritual Life*. In that year (1926) the valley of Ampezzo was still green and rustic, with only a few roofs clustering about the church, with its noble spire. The peasants were ideal peasants and the strangers very few, and true lovers of nature.

Cortina had extraneous advantages for me as well; it could be easily reached, yet not so easily as by a night express direct from Rome. It was almost inevitable to stop in Venice; and I fell into the habit of stopping there for some weeks in each year, especially in September and October. The fashion in Venice had moved to the Lido, where I didn't follow it; and the sea front, the Piazza and the Piazzetta preserved an Italian rather than a cosmopolitan character. I found a book by an old-fashioned English resident on *Walks in Venice* with accurate little maps indicating the turns to take at each point in the labyrinth of lanes; and with this guide I walked all over Venice, without ever taking a gondola, except on my arrival and departure, when I had luggage. The eye was feasted in Venice as nowhere else on light and colour. The sea, most inhuman of elements, met in perfect friendship here with the soft and pleasure-loving side of man; and the mixed architecture of a by-gone plutocracy reconciled me to the experiments of to-day.

Here too the desire to be splendid is in evidence, rather than vital greatness betrayed by a splendour that was unintended. How different these palaces, so rich and ornamental outside, so evi-

dently striving to outshine one another, from the severe grandeur
of the palaces of Rome, each turned inwards, walled and barred
like a castle or a monastery against the outer world, plain like a
fortress or a prison, yet imposing by the scale of the monumental
doors and spaced windows, the cliff-like walls and the defiant
cornices! In Venice, originally on the human scale, all was pleasant
loggias and balconies, where the gay inmates might crowd to see
and to be seen. Business was not hidden; it might be transacted in
the great Piazza or on the frequented Rialto; but Pleasure soon
drove it indoors, into the secret cabinets of rich men, while the
young and gallant paraded the squares or the Grand Canal, to
display their finery and plot their amours. Venice would have been
vulgar but for two blessed accidents, that made it inimitably beautiful. One was the magic of that lagoon on which it seemed to
float, and that mesh of canals vivifying it as the veins vivify the
body and everywhere mirroring a sky itself softened and dyed by
the denser tints that earth and water have reflected back upon it.
The other happy accident was the age in which Venice flourished
and from which it borrowed its arts. The model at first was Byzan-
tium, also a commercial city, although an oriental and hieratic
one; so that everything, even nautical things, came to the Venetians already mellowed and refined by the traditions of many ages
and many empires. These Venetians were *nouveaux riches*; they
could never have developed their arts from within; but they had
many contacts, such as other Christian nations generally lacked,
and they could adopt and combine many fashions, not without a
festive originality in combining them. So later, when it became
the fashion in Italy to be classical, the Venetians again had models
nobler than their own genius; yet these models gained a new
charm and elegance when reproduced, on a smaller scale, in the
incomparable stage-setting of Venice.

I lodged habitually at Danieli's, going out to Martini's by the
*Teatro Fenice* for luncheon, because it was quiet and pleasant
there at that hour, sitting under an awning in the well-paved
square, with interesting facades before one, and not too much

food, as happened then in good hotels. For dinner I usually went
to the Olympia, where a table at the back was reserved for me;
and when the band began to play at nine o'clock, I was ready to
go and stand in the Piazza, or walk about in the upper end of it,
where few people gathered. The public seems to think that to
hear music is to see the musicians fiddle and blow. I preferred not
to see them. Here, and on the Pincio in Rome, I had my only
taste of instrumental music: shocking confession, no doubt, for a
person supposed to relish the fine arts. But music bores me if I am
sitting penned in among a crowd in a hot place, with bright artificial lights, and a general pretence at intelligent interest, whether
such interest exists or not. It is too much like sitting through a
service in a Protestant church. At the opera I can forget this
discomfort because the impression, visual as well as auditory, is
violent enough to hold my attention; but for pure music I desire
the open air, solitude if possible, and liberty to move about and
to go away. There is a wonderful sense of freedom in standing on
one's two legs. It adds, in my feeling, to the sincere enjoyment of
both nature and art. Music and landscape then come as a gift, not
as a thing procured for a ticket that constitutes a promise and
imposes a sort of pledge. I prefer that the beautiful should come
upon me unannounced, and that it should leave me at liberty.*

At Danieli's my favourite room was a little one in the entresol,
No. 8, close over the entrance, where I could sit during my writing
hours in the morning and during my reading hours in the early
afternoon, by my low-silled window, open but discreetly curtained,
little above the level of the Riva degli Schiavoni. Here I was conscious of the life of the place but not disturbed by it, and re-
freshed, whenever I looked up, by the lovely picture of San
Giorgio Maggiore across the Bacino di San Marco. If I stretched
my neck a little, I could also see the Dogana and the domes and
belfry of La Salute; but this, although more ornate, seemed to me

---

* Veniam subito, nec quisquam nuntiet ante,
  sed videar caelo missus adesse tibi.
  Tibullus, III, *ad finem.*

less beautiful than San Giorgio, less naturally perfect and individual; because the brick and marble harmonies of San Giorgio, with the green roof of the tower, were a happy gift of fortune. Doubtless the plutocratic rebuilders of the old convent and hospital would have liked to face everything with white marble; but the rich, on their lavish scale, are no less or even more hampered than the poor; and in this case they had the exquisite taste of Palladio to redeem and to glorify their comparative poverty. The new west front should be shining white, to be gilded and mellowed by the setting sun; while the walls, the dome, and the outlying low buildings should preserve their weathered pink with only touches of white and grey in the lintels and cornices. And fortune smiled again when the campanile was added, a slender and more graceful copy of that of Saint Mark's, *matre pulchra filia pulchrior*: for it completes the harmony of its church, as the great campanile does not, lends it height and unity, rhymes the same russet with the same white, and caps the whole, in the hood of the spire, with a touch of aerial green. So nature has blessed and adopted this work of art, as if it had descended like a vision from the clouds and remained suspended between the sparkling sea and the depths of air.

Once, in 1939–40, when the Hotel Bristol in Rome was closed and about to be rebuilt, I spent a whole winter in Venice, not a thing to be recommended; yet a pleasant walk had just been opened along the sea front uninterruptedly to the Public Gardens. There were nine little bridges, I counted some 400 steps, to go up and down on the way: but from each bridge there was a new vista, and the varied shipping carried the mind from ancient wars to the one then beginning, and from those placid lagoons to the Southern Seas.

In Rome fortune at first lent me a living guide, in the person of the Rev. Luciano Zampa of Gubbio, a modernist priest who had translated my *Egotism in German Philosophy*. It was with him that I first ventured into Italian conversation. He helped me without discouraging me by too many corrections; and I could always put in an English or Spanish or French or even Latin word if my Italian failed me. Besides, he could often guess what I wished to say before I quite said it; my later friend Michele Petrone used to do the same; and with these two I could even become eloquent in Italian, in spite of my insecure hold on the language. But the great service that Zampa did me was to show me the less obvious sights of Rome. Being a provincial priest—at first dressed as a lay-man, having been unfrocked for his modernism, but afterwards restored to his clerical privileges—he had a traditional admiration for all that was ecclesiastically important. Great ancient columns and rich marbles inspired him with respect, apart from their beauty: and this proprietory human esteem for the arts was a good corrective to the priggish aestheticism of my English-speaking artis-tic friends. Later some of these artistic friends—Geoffrey Scott, for instance, in Florence—abetted this ecclesiastical view in so far as they renounced pre-Raphaelism and learned to love the baroque; but that was an aesthetic fashion also, and corrupt; Aubrey Beardsley substituted for Burne-Jones; whereas my honest Zampa was simply impressed by the positive qualities of great size, rarity, cost or splendour.

In spite of these lessons, however, I soon retreated into my aesthetic, or rather my poetic, shell, and limited my diet of visual impressions to a few chosen sights. The central streets came in inevitably for a person who lives in them and frequents cafés; but my usual walk was to Trinità de' Monti, the Pincio and the Villa Borghese. On some days I would go instead to the Tiber, St. Peter's, and (when it was made) the admirable garden at Castel Sant'Angelo; or else to the Janiculum, San Pietro in Mon-torio and, above all, the Aqua Paola, where I always read the monumental inscription over the fountain, until finally I knew it by heart. And if any friends turned up, I would explain my aver-sion to museums and picture galleries, but would offer to take them, after luncheon, to see three things, the Pantheon, Michel-angelo's Moses, and the Forum from the top of the Capitoline, which included admiring the two pavilions of Michelangelo and the statue of Marcus Aurelius. Of these things I never tired; but of seeing more things or other things I had had enough. Fresher thought came and I could transmit more pleasure in recognising these old objects than in staring at new ones.

Yet when not compelled to talk or to avoid useless explorations, I took many other casual turns in the labyrinth of the old streets: sometimes purposely making little circuits in search of odd variations on the theme of doors and windows, not to speak of church fronts and of fountains. Sometimes lovely things turned up in this way: for instance the German burying ground by the Sacristy of St. Peter's, and the court of the hospital adjoining the church in the Borgo Santo Spirito, not far distant. Monte Cavallo, at the tip of the Quirinal, where also a band played, was another spot to loiter in at sunset, when the level light gilded the whole length of the Alta Semita as far as the Porta Pia, a caprice of Michelangelo. Many things depended on the time of day and the weather for their full effect, as landscape necessarily does; and great weathered works of architecture become part of the landscape and move the mind to poetry, not to pedantic criticism.

This for me, with my imperfect eyesight wrapping everything in a second often merciful atmosphere, applies even to interiors. With Spanish preconceptions of what a church should be—sombre, devotional, and rich in shrines—Italian interiors are apt to strike me as empty and cold; and even the great basilicas in Rome seem to lack a focus and to be too much like artist's models and too little like places of worship. But this may be due to personal prejudice, which a new personal experience may correct. Now (1942) that I live not far from the Lateran, I often cross San Giovanni, as I used to do the Cathedral of Avila, in order to avoid the hot sun on the rough pavement; and being old and fond of sitting upon public benches, I rest for a moment on one of the wooden seats that are found there (but not, alas, at St. Peter's); and in those calm moments my eye has learned to frame wonderful vistas in that great church, forward to the restored apse with its golden mosaics and its papal throne, or across aisles and aisles, into vast side chapels, each a church in itself. And then the whole place seems to lose its rigidity and its dead pomp, and to become a marvellous labyrinth, as if it were a work of nature or of fancy rather than of human art. The gigantic violent Apostles in the nave cease to seem monstrous; they become baroque works of nature, as if water by chance had molded the sides of a cliff into the likeness of Titans. And what might have disappointed in the mother of Cathedrals, the moderate height, becomes only the condition of unlimited breadth; and you cannot complain that in the centre you have a ceiling instead of a vault or a soaring dome, when you see beyond, quite subordinate to this rectangular space, soaring domes and vaults, enclosing other spaces and shedding variously coloured lights on other elaborate altars. Thus familiarity discloses the richness of what seemed bare at first glance, and you find amplitude, time, and silence intensely present in what you had passed by as insignificant.

It might seem that with age places gained upon persons in interest to my mind; and that my pleasure grew in intercourse with things rather than with ideas. Yet what held me in things was only their aspects, the picturesque or moral suggestions in them; for to things as material weights or forces I have never become attached. The old animal passion for fetishes, for hugging and hoarding particular objects because of their material identity, seems to have been entirely extinct in me; and it was precisely this indifference to physical identities that made me episodical in friendship and Platonising in love. I was far from inconsistent or variable in affection towards the *true* objects of my choice, but these were not the material things or persons that chance put in my way, in their necessarily mixed and changing composition. I saw only the gifts and virtues of which, perhaps for the first time, they gave me a clear idea. They become to that extent my local shrines or the saints for that day in my calendar; but never did the places or the persons turn into idols for my irrational worship. It was only the *numen* in them that I loved, who, as I passed by abstracted, whispered some immortal word in my ear.

It is true that persons, however changed in aspect, at least keep their memories. They may hark back to the scenes and the interests that may have bound them once to their old friends; and beneath memory there is also a soul, an innate disposition and character that may be recognised at moments in spite of all the incrustations of age, servitude and vice. And besides that, there are lessons of experience; acquirements and remunerations brought about by fortune, that sometimes transform the most commonplace persons, or the least prepossessing originally, into noble minds; and then the Holy Ghost, that is no respecter of persons, speaks to us through those so softened and pathetic masks. I would not nurse my animal aversions any more than my animal favouritisms. Without disowning in any way the bonds of blood or of comradeship or of social utility, I gladly recognise the good and the beautiful in unexpected quarters; and I am not in the least daunted in my cult of those divine essences when I find that they have disappeared from a place or a person that had once seemed to possess them.

Never have I enjoyed youth so thoroughly as I have in my old age. In writing *Dialogues in Limbo, The Last Puritan,* and now all these descriptions of the friends of my youth and the young friends of my middle age, I have drunk the pleasure of life more pure, more joyful, than it ever was when mingled with all the hidden anxieties and little annoyances of actual living. Nothing is inherently and invincibly young except spirit. And spirit can enter a human being perhaps better in the quiet of old age and dwell there more undisturbed than in the turmoil of adventure. But it must be in solitude. I do not need or desire to hob-nob artificially with other old men in order to revisit them in their salad days, and to renew my own. In Rome, in the eternal city, I feel nearer to my own past, and to the whole past and future of the world, than I should in any cemetery or in any museum of relics. Old places and old persons in their turn, when spirit dwells in them, have an intrinsic vitality of which youth is incapable; precisely the balance and wisdom that comes from long perspec-

tives and broad foundations. Everything shines then for the spirit
by its own light in its own place and time; but not as it shone
in its own restless eyes. For in its own eyes each person and each
place was the centre of a universe full of threatening and tempting things; but old age, having less intensity at the centre has
more clearness at the circumference, and knows that just because
spirit, at each point, is a private centre for all things, no one point,
no one phase of spirit is materially a public centre for all the rest.
Thus recognition and honour flow out to all things, from the
mind that conceives them justly and without egotism; and thus
mind is reconciled to its own momentary existence and limited
vision by the sense of the infinite supplements that embosom it
on every side.

# CHAPTER VIII

## *EPILOGUE: MY HOST THE WORLD*

PERSONS and places people the world; they individuate its parts; and I have devoted this book to recording some of them that remain alive in my memory. Mine are insignificant recollections: for even when the themes happen to have some importance as persons and places in the great world, it is not at all in that capacity that I prize and describe them. I keep only some old miniature or some little perspective that caught my eye in passing, when the persons perhaps were young and the places empty and not dressed up to receive visitors, as are museums, libraries, ball-rooms and dinner-tables. Those were free glimpses of the world that I could love and could carry away. They were my consolations.

Yet the very contrast between these glimpses, all picturesque and aerial, and the vast obscure inexorable world from which they came, forced me gradually to form some notion of that material world also. Mine was a blue sea family: our world was that of colonial officials and great merchants. From the beginning I learned to think of the earth as a globe with its surface chiefly salt water, a barren treacherous and intractable waste for mankind, yet tempting and beautiful and swarming with primitive animals not possible to tame or humanise but sometimes good to eat. In fine, I opened my eyes on the world with the conviction that it was inhuman: not meant for man, but habitable by him, and possible to exploit, with prudence, in innumerable ways: a conviction that everything ever since has confirmed.

One peculiarity seemed common to all satisfactions: they brought something perfect, consummate, final. The sea, after no matter what storms, returned to its equilibrium and placidity; its gamut was definite. Voyages all led to some port. The vastness and violence of nature, in challenging and often decimating mankind, by no means tend to dehumanise it. The quality of attainable goods may change with the conditions for attaining them; but the way is always open, at the right time, for the right sort of animal and for the right sort of mind. Arts have their dates; and the great question is not what age you live in or what art you pursue but what perfection you can achieve in that art under those circumstances.

The great master of sympathy with nature, in my education, was Lucretius. Romantic poets and philosophers, when they talk of nature, mean only landscape or other impressions due to aerial perspectives, sensuous harmonies of colour or form, or vital intoxications, such as those of riding, sea-faring, or mountain-climbing. Nature is loved for heightening self-consciousness and prized for ministering to human comfort and luxury, but is otherwise ignored as contemptible, dead, or non-existent. Or when people's temper is hardy and pugnacious, they may require nature as a buffer on which to rain their mighty blows and carve their important initials. Where human strength comes from or what ends human existence might serve, they neither know nor care.

The spirit in me felt itself cast upon this social and political world somewhat like Robinson Crusoe upon his island. We were both creatures of the same Great Nature; and my world, in its geography and astronomy, like Robinson Crusoe's island, had much more massive and ancient foundations than the small utterly insecure waif that had been wrecked upon it. In its social and political structure, however, my world was more like Crusoe's energetic person: for my island was densely inhabited: an ugly town, a stinted family, a common school; and the most troublesome and inescapable of its denizens was the particular body in which my spirit found itself rooted; so rooted that it became doubtful whether that body with its feelings and actions was not my true self, rather than this invisible spirit which they oppressed. I seemed to be both; and yet this compulsive and self-tormenting creature called "Me" was more odious and cruel to the "I" within than were the sea and sky, the woods and mountains, or the very cities and crowds of people that this animal "Me" moved among: for the spirit in me was happy and free ranging through that world, but troubled and captive in its close biological integument.

This is the double conflict, the social opposition and the moral agony, that spirit suffers by being incarnate; and yet if it were not incarnate it could not be individual, with a situation in space and time, a language and special perspective over nature and history: indeed, if not incarnate, spirit could not *exist* at all or be the inner light and perpetual witness of *life* in its dramatic vicissitudes.

If it be the fate of all spirit to live in a special body and a special age, and yet, for its vocation and proper life, to be addressed from that centre to all life and to all being, I can understand why I have been more sensible to this plight and to this mission than were most of my contemporaries. For by chance I was a foreigner where I was educated; and although the new language and customs interested me and gave me no serious trouble, yet speculatively and emotionally, especially in regard to religion, the world around me was utterly undigestible. The times also were moving, rapidly and exultingly, towards what for me was chaos and universal triviality. At first these discords sounded like distant thunder. Externally they were not yet violent; the world smiled in my eyes as I came to manhood, and the beauties and dignity of the past made the present unimportant. And as the feeling of being a stranger and an exile by nature as well as by accident grew upon me in time, it came to be almost a point of pride; some people may have thought it an affectation. It was not that; I have always admired the normal child of his age and country. My case was humanly unfortunate and involved many defects; yet it opened to me another vocation, not better (I admit no absolute standards) but more speculative, freer, juster, and for me happier.

I had always dreamt of travel, and it was oftenest in the voluntary, interested, appreciative rôle of the traveller that I felt myself most honest in my dealings with my environment. The world was My Host; I was a temporary guest in his busy and animated establishment. We met as strangers; yet each had generic and well-grounded ideas of what could be expected of the other. First impressions made these expectations more precise; the inn was habitable; the guest was presumably solvent. We might prove mutually useful. My Host and I could become friends, diplomatically; but we were not akin in either our interests or our powers. The normal economy of an innkeeper, though incidentally and in a measure it supplies the wants of his guests, knows nothing of their private moral economy. Their tastes in wines, in service, or in music may entirely outrun or contradict his long-established practice, which he will impose on his guests with all the authority of a landlord; and there may not be another inn in the place, or only worse ones. The guest has no right to demand what is not provided. He must be thankful for any little concessions that may be made to his personal tastes, if he is tactful and moderate in his requirements, pays his bills promptly and gives decent tips.

Such at least was the case in the nineteenth century when the world made itself pleasant to the traveller; and not to rich travellers only but to the most modest, and even to the very poor in their little purchases and popular feasts. Personal freedom produced a certain dignity and good humour even in bargaining; for to buy and sell, to patronise a shop or a boarding-house, was an act of kindness; and bills, at least in civilly commercial England, were always receipted "with thanks." Having lived a peaceful independent life, free from hardship or misfortune, I have found it easy to conform externally with the mechanism of society. Matter has been kind to me, and I am a lover of matter. Not only aesthetically but dynamically, as felt by Lucretius, nature to me is a welcome presence; and modern progress in mechanical invention and industrial luxury has excited joyously my materialistic imagination, as it did prophetically that of Bacon. Moreover, I inherited from my father a bond with matter which Bacon and Lucretius probably did not feel: the love of employing leisure in small mechanical occupations. I should never have read and written so much if the physical side of these employments had not been congenial to me and rich with a quiet happiness. Any common surroundings and any commonplace people pleased me well enough; it was only when sugary rapture was demanded about them or by them, as happened almost everywhere in my youth, that my stomach rose in radical protest. Then I discovered how much the human world of my time had become the enemy of spirit and therefore of its own light and peace.

How had this happened? Not at all as lovers of antiquity or of the middle ages seem to think, because of mechanical inventions or natural sciences or loss of Christian faith. These transformations might all have occurred in the normal growth of society. Variety in cultures is not due to aberrations any more than is the variety of animal species. But there may be aberration in any species or any culture when it becomes *vicious*; that is, when it forms habits destructive of its health and of its ability to prosper in its environment. Now modern sciences and inventions are not vicious in this sense; on the contrary, they bring notable additions to human *virtù*. And I think that the Renaissance, with the historical learning and humanism which it fostered, was also a great gain for human happiness and self-knowledge. Of this the surface of the modern world during my youth gave continual evidence, in spite of an undercurrent of unrest and disaffection sometimes heard rumbling below. "My Host's" establishment made a brave appearance; and I was particularly conscious of many new facilities of travel, breadth of information, and cosmopolitan convenience and luxury. Though there was no longer any dignity in manners, or much distinction in costume, fashion had not lost all its charm. In literature and the fine arts talent could give pleasure by its expertness, if not by its taste or savour. I have described how in Boston and in England I sometimes sipped at the rim of the plutocratic cup; and this was a real pleasure, because beneath the delicacy of the material feast there was a lot of shrewd experience in that society, and of placid kindness.

There was another cosmopolitan circle, however, less select and less worldly, but no less entertaining and no less subject to fashion and to ironical gossip, the Intellectuals, into whose company I was sometimes drawn. I was officially one of them, yet they felt in their bones that I might be secretly a traitor. "Ah, yes," cried a distinguished Jesuit recently when I was casually mentioned, "he is the *poetical* atheist." And an Italian professor, also a Catholic but tinged with German idealism, remarked of me: "the trouble with him is that he has never succeeded in outgrowing material-ism." Finally, a faithful diehard of British psychologism, asked why I was overlooked among contemporary philosophers, replied: "Because he has no originality. Everything in him is drawn from Plato and Leibnitz." This critical band is democratic in that it recognises no official authority and lets fluid public opinion carry the day; yet it is, on principle, in each man, private and inde-pendent in judgment. Few, however, have much time to read originals or to study facts. Leaders and busybodies must obey their momentum. A personal reaction on what other people say is so-cially sufficient; it will do for the press; and it will corroborate the critic's opinion in his own eyes.

I cannot overcome a settled distrust of merely intellectual accomplishment, militant in the void. I prefer common virtues and current beliefs, even if intellectually prejudiced and simple, when the great generative order of nature has bred them, and lent them its weight and honesty. For I do not rebel in the least at political and moral mutations when this same generative order brings them about spontaneously; for it is then on the side of change that clear intelligence discerns the lesser danger and the wider inter-ests. I should have loved the Gracchi; but not the belated Cato or the belated Brutus. All four were martyrs; but the first two spoke for the poor, for the suffering half of the people, oppressed by a shortsighted power that neglected its responsibilities; while the last two were conceited ideologues, jealous of their traditional rights, and utterly blind to destiny. If I were not too old and could venture to write in French, I should compose a short history of *Les Faux Pas de la Philosophie*; by which title I should not refer to *innocent* errors, with which all human speculation must be infected, nor to the symbolic or mythological form of the wisest wisdom, but only to militant heresies and self-contradictions due to wilful conceit, individual or tribal, verbal or moral; and there is little in European philosophy that is not infected with these *unnecessary* errors. Let the reader compose his own catalogue of these blind alleys explored by the ancients and by the moderns; since this is a biographical book, I will limit myself to the first and principal *Faux Pas* that the world has seemed to me to have taken in my time.

The contemporary world has turned its back on the attempt and even on the desire to live reasonably. The two great wars (so far) of the twentieth century were adventures in enthusiastic unreason. They were inspired by unnecessary and impracticable ambitions; and the "League" and the "United Nations," feebly set up by the victors, were so irrationally conceived that they at once reduced their victory to a stalemate. What is required for living rationally? I think the conditions may be reduced to two: First, self-knowledge, the Socratic key to wisdom; and second, sufficient knowledge of the world to perceive what alternatives are open to you and which of them are favourable to your true interests.

Now the contemporary world has plenty of knowledge of nature for its purposes, but its purposes show a positively insane abandonment of its true interests. You may say that the proletariat knows its interests perfectly; they are to work less and to earn more. Those are indeed its interests so long as it remains a proletariat: but to be a proletariat is an inhuman condition. Proletarians are human beings, and their first interest is to have a home, a family, a chosen trade, and freedom in practising it. And more particularly a man's true interest may exceptionally be not to have those things, but to wander alone like the rhinoceros; or perhaps to have a very special kind of home, family and occupation. There must be freedom of movement and vocation. There must be *Lebensraum* for the spirit.

There have always been beggars and paupers in the world, because there is bound to be a margin of the unfit, too bad or too good to keep in step with any well organised society; but that the great body of mankind should sink into a proletariat has been an unhappy effect of the monstrous growth of cities, made possible by the concentration of trade and the multiplication of industries, mechanised, and swelling into monopolies.

The natural state of mankind, before foreign conquerors dominate it or native ideologues reform it, is full of incidental evils; prophets have ample cause for special denunciations and warnings; yet there is, as in all animal economy, a certain nucleus of self-preserving instincts and habits, a normal constitution of society. Nature with its gods is the landlord of whose fields and woods they are local and temporary tenants; and with this invincible power they make prudent and far-seeing covenants. They know what is for their good and by what arts it might be secured. They live by agriculture, the hunting or breeding of animals, and such domestic arts as their climate and taste lead them to cultivate; and when a quarrel arises among them, or with strangers, they battle to preserve or to restore their free life, without more ambitious intentions. They are materially and morally rooted in the earth, bred in one land or one city. They are *civilised*. Wandering nations, with nothing of their own and working havoc wherever they go, are *barbarians*. Such "barbarians" were the proletariat of antiquity. When they occupied some civilised region without exterminating the natives, and established in the old strongholds a permanent foreign domination, they became half-civilised themselves, without shedding altogether the predatory and adventurous practices of their ancestors. This is the compound origin and nature of modern Western governments.

Varied, picturesque, and romantic mixtures of civilisation beneath and barbarism above have filled the history of Christendom, and produced beautiful transient arts, in which there was too

little wisdom and too much fancy and fashion: think of Gothic
architecture, or of manners, dress, poetry, and philosophy from
the middle ages to our day. Civilisation had become more enter-
prising, plastic, and irresponsible, while barbarism seemed to retreat into sports, and into legal extravagances in thought and
action. Intellectual chaos and political folly could thus come to
co-exist strangely with an irresistible dominance of mechanical
industry. The science that served this industrial progress by no
means brought moral enlightenment. It merely enlarged acquaintance with phenomena and enabled clever inventors to construct
all sorts of useful or superfluous machines. At first perhaps it was
expected that science would make all mankind both rich and free
from material cares (two contradictory hopes) and would at the
same time enlighten them at last about the nature of things,
including their own nature, so that adequate practical wisdom
would be secured together with fabulous material well-being.

This is the dream of the moderns, on which I found My Host
boastfully running his establishment. He expected his guests also
to act accordingly and to befuddle and jollify one another, so that
all should convince themselves that they were perfectly happy and
should advertise their Host's business wherever they went. Such
forced enterprise, forced confidence, and forced satisfaction would
never have sprung from domestic arts or common knowledge
spontaneously extended. It was all artificial and strained, marking
the inhuman domination of some militant class or sect. This
society lacked altogether that essential trait of rational living, to
have a clear, sanctioned, ultimate aim. The cry was for vacant
freedom and indeterminate progress: *Vorwärts! Avanti! Onward!
Full speed ahead!* without asking whether directly before you
was not a bottomless pit.

This has been the peculiar malady of my times. I saw the outbreak of it in my boyhood, and I have lived to see what seem
clear symptoms of its end. The Great Merchants of my parents'
youth had known nothing of it on their blue-sea voyages round
Cape Horn or the Cape of Good Hope. Their good hope had

been to amass a great fortune in fifteen or twenty years, and return home to bring up a blooming family in splendour and peace. They foresaw an orderly diffused well-being spreading out from them over all mankind. The fountains of happiness were ready to flow in every heart and mind if only people were suffered to have their own way materially and socially. That the masses would crowd out, exclude, indoctrinate, enslave, and destroy one another could not cross their genial and innocent minds, as they skimmed those immense oceans in their tight, strictly disciplined, white-sailed little craft.

Alas! The healthy growth of science and commerce had been crossed, long before the rise of the Great Merchants, by an insidious moral and political revolution. From the earliest times there have been militant spirits not content with inevitable changes and with occasional wars between neighbouring states, not usually wars of conquest or eternal hatred, but collisions in readjusting the political equilibrium between nations when their actual relations were no longer the same. Indeed, the tragic causes of conflict and ruin in civilizations are fundamentally internal to each society. A whole city or state may sometimes be destroyed, like Carthage: but history, then, comes to an end for that particular society, and the others continue their course as if their vanished rival had never existed. This course may be cut short, however, by internal disruption and suicidal revolutions. Every generation is born as ignorant and wilful as the first man; and when tradition has lost its obvious fitness or numinous authority, eager minds will revert without knowing it to every false hope and blind alley that had tempted their predecessors long since buried under layer upon layer of ruins. And these eager minds may easily become leaders; for society is never perfect; grievances and misfortunes perpetually breed rebellion in the oppressed heart; and the eloquent imagination of youth and of indignation will find the right words to blow the discontent, always smouldering, into sudden flame. Often things as they are become intolerable; there must be insurrection at any cost, as when the estab-

lished order is not only casually oppressive, but ideally perverse
and due to some previous epidemic of militant madness become
constitutional. Against that domination, established in wilful indifference to the true good of man and to his possibilities, any
political nostrum, proposed with the same rashness, will be accepted with the same faith. Thus the blind in extirpating the
mad may plant a new madness.

That this is the present state of the world everyone can see
by looking about him, or reading the newspapers; but I think that
the elements in this crisis have been working in the body-politic
for ages; ever since the Reformation, not to say since the age of
the Greek Sophists and of Socrates. For the virulent cause of
this long fever is subjectivism, egotism, conceit of mind. Not
that culture of the conscience and even the logical refinements
of dialectic are anything but good for the mind itself and for
moral self-knowledge, which is one of the two conditions that
I have assigned to political sanity; but the same logical arts are
fatal if they are used to construct, by way of a moral fable, an
anthropomorphic picture of the universe given out for scientific
truth and imposed on mankind by propaganda, by threats, and
by persecution. And this militant method of reforming mankind
by misrepresenting their capacities and their place in the universe
is no merely ancient or mediaeval delusion. It is the official and
intolerant method of our most zealous contemporary prophets and
reformers. Barbarism has adopted the weapons of flattery and
prophecy. Merciless irrational ambition has borrowed the language
of brotherly love.

The very fact, however, that these evils have deep roots and
have long existed without destroying Western civilisation, but on
the contrary have stimulated its contrary virtues and confused
arts—this very fact seems to me to counsel calmness in contem-
plating the future. Those who look for a panacea will not find it.
Those who advise resignation to a life of industrial slavery (because spiritual virtues may be cultivated by a slave, like Epictetus,
more easily perhaps than by rich men) are surrendering the

political future to an artificial militant regime that cannot last unaltered for a decade anywhere, and could hardly last a day, if by military force it were ever made universal. The fanaticism of all parties must be allowed to burn down to ashes, like a fire out of control. If it survives, it will be only because it will have humanised itself, reduced its dogmas to harmless metaphors, and sunk down a tap-root, to feed it, into the dark damp depths of mother earth. The economy of nature includes all particular movements, combines and transforms them all, but never diverts its wider processes to render them obedient to the prescriptions of human rhetoric. Things have their day, and their beauties in that day. It would be preposterous to expect any one civilisation to last forever.

Had it happened in my time (as by chance it did happen) that my landlord should give me notice that he was about to pull down his roof over my head, I might have been a little troubled for a moment; but presently I should have begun to look for other lodgings not without a certain curious pleasure, and probably should have found some (as I did, and better ones) in which to end my days. So, I am confident, will the travelling Spirit do—this ever-renewed witness, victim, and judge of existence, divine yet born of woman. Obediently it will learn other affections in other places, unite other friends, and divide other peoples; and the failure of over-exact hopes and overweening ambitions will not prevent spirit from continually turning the passing virtues and sorrows of nature into glimpses of eternal truth.

# INDEX

# INDEX